Am I the Only Crazy Mom on This Planet?

Am I the Only Crazy Mom on This Planet?

Elizabeth Cody Newenhuyse

ZondervanPublishingHouse
Grand Rapids, Michigan

A Division of HarperCollinsPublishers

Am I the Only Crazy Mom on This Planet?
Copyright © 1994 by Elizabeth Cody Newenhuyse
All rights reserved

Zondervan Publishing House
Grand Rapids, Michigan 49530

Library of Congress Cataloging-in-Publication Data

Newenhuyse, Elizabeth Cody.
    Am I the only crazy mom on this planet? / Elizabeth Cody
Newenhuyse.
        p.   cm.
    ISBN 0-310-38631-4
    1. Newenhuyse, Elizabeth Cody. 2. Mothers—United States—
Biography. 3. Family—United States. 4. Family—Religious life.
I. Title.
HQ759.N53   1994
306.874'3'0207—dc20   93–41062
                                                                CIP

Edited by Mary McCormick
Designed by Gary Colby
Cover design by Jody Langley

94 95 96 97 98 / DH / 7 6 5 4 3 2 1

To Amanda

Contents

Thank God that we do not have to write books entirely alone. If that were the case, I would not only be crazy but clueless and probably somewhat peculiar. Therefore I want to thank some people who played, knowingly or not, special roles in bringing this book to you, my reader and friend:

My editor, Lyn Cryderman. Lyn is a man who appreciates both humor and excellence. I appreciate his encouraging me to strive for both here.

My publisher, Scott Bolinder, one of the truly good guys in Christian publishing.

Jean Bloom, Mary McCormick, Christine Anderson, and the rest of the Zondervan team.

Faith Covenant Church, my spiritual lifeline. Special thanks to Charlotte Madeliene Mesimore, Bobette Gustafson, Dori Wine, Emily Wolgemuth, and Judy Anderson.

Everyone who prayed that I could actually do this.

My mother, Beverly Cody; my mother-in-law, Betty Newenhuyse; my beloved husband, Fritz; and, of course, my daughter, Amanda.

Introduction

*T*here are days when I don't know where I'd be without a sense of humor. You know those days—you wake up with a pounding headache, and things go downhill from there. The dishwasher backs up, the dog gets sick over your just-cleaned carpeting, the school calls to tell you that your kid socked another child on the playground and could you come in for a conference? Your best friend calls to tell you that she just reached her ideal weight. By this time *you* are ready to dive back under the covers and not come out until Kevin Costner shows up at the back door with a dozen roses.

Thank God for the gift of laughter. God must have loved us very much to give us humor. It's as if He's telling us that this, too, shall pass—and maybe we'd all be a lot better off if we lighten up, step back, and ask ourselves if the things that drive us moms crazy are really that important.

I'm a mom. And a wife. And (theoretically) a homemaker. I spend my days juggling school stuff and church stuff, doing a bit of writing here and there, postponing the ironing, and looking for nylons that don't have runs in the feet.

I like to laugh, and I like to learn. I hope that you do, too, because that's what this book is all about—some funny stories to maybe lighten your load a little, some insights to inspire and encourage you, some "girlfriend" talk to help you see that you're not alone. Most of all, in these stressed-out times, this book is a reminder that there is much in life to love and laugh at and feel good about . . . and praise our good God for that!

Elizabeth Cody Newenhuyse

A DAY WITH MOM

S even A.M. Stumble out of bed. Grope blindly for bath-robe. Note that robe has dried spot where sniffling child used it for handkerchief.

7:03 A.M. Drink coffee. Look at to-do list and remember that I promised to bring Rice Krispies treats for church club party. Search in cupboard for marshmallows. Wonder if ancient jar of dark molasses could be substituted. Wonder if spilled molasses attracts ants.

7:15 A.M. Shower. Pray in shower. Discover that the highlighting-conditioner bottle is empty. Recall that conditioner was used on Barbies ("I'm playing salon"). Resign self to dingy-hair day.

7:37 A.M. Phone rings. Answer phone half-dressed. Neighbor child needs ride to school. Neighbor child cannot tell time and wants to come over right away. Stall neighbor child.

7:48 A.M. Apply makeup. Phone rings. Stab self in eye with mascara wand. Answer phone with eye streaming. "How are you today, Mrs. Newenhyzee? This is Michael," says ingratiating salesman, mispronouncing my name. "FINE!" I bark.

8:00 A.M. Try to wake Amanda. "Time for school, honey." Amanda opens one eye.

8:15 A.M. Neighbor child shows up. Neighbor child wants

to play *March of the Merry Mice* for me on violin. Stall neighbor child. Husband excuses himself, saying he has important things to attend to in garage.

8:19 A.M. Try to wake Amanda. Notice edge in my voice. Feel guilty. Start singing "Good Morning, Merry Sunshine." Amanda dives under covers. "Go away!"

8:22 A.M. Select clothes for Amanda—a plaid skirt and sweater with snowflake pattern. Amanda rejects in favor of pink Spandex stirrup pants and black sweatshirt. Gird self for argument. Recall being forced to wear embarrassing saddle shoes to school as a child. Give in.

8:40 A.M. Check on Amanda. She is sitting there with only her undershirt on, holding a headless Barbie. "I did an operation," she says. "I had to amplitate her head. Do people ever get new brains?" Stifle desire to scream, "YES, and I'm looking for an organ donor right now!"

Neighbor child is practicing violin in the next room. Reassess open-heart, open-home commitment.

8:57 A.M. Amanda reminds me that she needs a permission slip signed for a field trip, with a dollar for bus expense. Scrabble through yesterday's mail pile. Cannot find slip. Dig in kitchen garbage. Retrieve slip with coffee grounds clinging to it. Wipe slip and hope teacher understands the vicissitudes of motherhood. Borrow dollar from Amanda. Neighbor child stares at me. Begin muttering to self.

9:08 A.M. Depart for school with seven minutes to spare. Amanda runs to car holding piece of bacon. Her breakfast. Feel guilty. Consider making pot roast for her lunch to make up for inadequate morning meal. Husband emerges from garage looking chipper. Husband makes hearty remark: "Well, all ready for another big day?" Husband notices wife's stony silence and subsides.

9:12 A.M. Arrive at school. Park illegally. "Run!" I say.

Amanda turns. "I love you," she says. Feel guilty. "I love you, too, Sweets."

9:17 A.M. Alone at home. Pour self enormous cup of coffee and sit down, staring at kitchen mess. Mull returning to office job and hiring a nanny. Think of tax implications and reconsider. Observe ant crawling out from cupboard. Inspect molasses bottle. Molasses bottle is cemented to bottom of cabinet.

3:22 P.M. Stand in supermarket trying to decide between Chips Ahoy and Oreos for club treats.

3:38 P.M. Pick up Amanda. View Amanda's portrait of Franklin Pierce in classroom. Unable to distinguish between Franklin Pierce and another child's portrait of George Bush. Rave over Amanda's picture.

3:43 P.M. Greet mother who is picking up her child. Envy mother's slimness in jeans. Resolve to eat nothing but white tuna and broccoli until spring—beginning tomorrow.

3:55 P.M. Home. Inspect Amanda's school papers. Nothing to volunteer for, sign, pay, or remember. Thank God for small blessings.

4:00 P.M. Start browning pot roast.

4:15 P.M. Start boiling potatoes for mashing. Amanda's favorite.

4:23 P.M. Start scraping carrots for steaming. Amanda's favorite.

4:34 P.M. Start beating instant pudding. Etc.

4:45 P.M. Amanda comes into kitchen, holding doll amputee, looks suspiciously at stove and asks what's for dinner. I tell her and am unable to resist the reminder that the meal includes four things she will eat.

She hugs me. I hug her. Thank God for large blessings.

THE EASY WAY TO KEEP UP WITH THE JONESES

*T*here are some things you like to think you've outgrown. Acne, for one. Listening to music at deafening levels on headphones, for another. Peer pressure, for a third. After all, I am an adult. Married, a mother, a mature Christian, a taxpayer. I even have my own American Express card. Isn't that enough?

Not in our neighborhood.

Oh, the pressures are different from the pressures you experience when you are an adolescent. I've heard that our local middle school has "fashion police" who accost unwary classmates in the halls, sneering at them because they're wearing no-name K-Mart athletic shoes instead of Air Jordans or whatever the approved footwear is these days. When you're an adult, no one actually comes up to you in the parking lot at church, or work, and asks with lip curled, "Why are you driving that old Dodge Aries instead of a Camry?" or taunts you in the supermarket for buying tacky fish sticks (which your kids will eat) instead of broccoli (which they will not).

Grown-up peer pressure takes many forms, most of them infinitely subtle. You've got your everybody-drives-a-minivan-so-maybe-we-had-better-too pressure. You've got your my-child-started-Suzuki-at-age-three pressure. Your come-over-and-see-my-new-computer-setup pressure. How do I succumb to conformity? Let me count the ways.

Like I said, though, the neighbors are the worst.

We bought the house we're now living in partly because we loved the neighborhood. Older homes, big trees, walk to school, and train. Lots of Christians. Lots of families with children. Nicely kept houses and yards. Friendly. Desirable. The kind of neighborhood both my husband and I grew up in; the kind of neighborhood we wanted to raise our own family in . . .

Let's back up a moment to that "nicely kept."

All those green lawns, all that freshly painted trim, those colorful flower beds, and inviting Christmas lights don't just happen by themselves—they come at a price, and it is the price of *your* labor. Your *visible* labor. (They also come at the price of your spending real money, but we'll get to that.)

My husband and I are not what you would call compulsive about home and yard maintenance. Oh, we'll do it . . . eventually. The lawn does get mowed, the bushes pruned, the leaves raked, the snow shoveled. The half-off-its-hinges back storm door is put to rights, but it's not the first thing that comes to mind when we have time to kill: "We have an hour before we have to be at the church dinner." "Good! Let's paint the attic louvers!" We do what we have to do—no more, no less.

But, peer pressure being what it is, we have learned to put on a good facade. I will give you an example. Let's say it's a fine May Saturday and our family is just returning from a bike ride. We're sweaty and sore and all we really want to do is go sit on the front porch and drink lemonade. But up and down the block you can hear the vernal symphony of Toros and John Deeres tuning up. How would it *look* if we lounged slothfully about drinking highly-sugared liquids? No one wants to earn a reputation as the neighborhood wastrel. You know the kind—they keep their browning Christmas wreath up until the beginning of Lent; they use ugly metal garbage cans instead of those nice red ones from Ace; they let their dog just sort of stand around in the front yard instead of keeping it properly fenced up; their kids always seem to have Kool-Aid stains around their mouths. There's one on every block.

Well, that's not us. So this is what we do. One of our neighbors, the one who built an entire deck all by himself, is out thatching his lawn. The first thing I will do is pick up sticks, an easy way to look responsible. I'll strenuously bend and lift, bend and lift even the smallest twigs, until I have an impressive armload. Then I'll stagger over to the hidden area behind the garage where we've been collecting deadwood for five years, wait until I'm sure I'm in the punctilious neighbor's line of sight, and wave, still with the stick bundle in my arms. I'll call out something really obvious like "Lots of work in the spring, eh, Floyd?" (Not his real name.) He'll nod and smile and go back to his raking. Can't beat the clubby camaraderie of these spring Saturdays.

After dumping the sticks, I'll see my husband on his way into the house for a lemonade refill. I intercept him with a loud "Fritz, did you change the plugs in the mower?" and Fritz, ever a quick study, will yell back, "No, I gotta go get a file to sharpen the blades!" He comes back out and heads into the garage, where he bangs about and sounds really intentional. Actually, he is in there LOOKING for the mower under the snowblowers he picked up at someone's garage sale and tried to use last winter, only when he got them he didn't notice they lacked starter cords. At least we mean well.

But, as they say, the road to dereliction is paved with good intentions and dandelions. We have neighbors who have no weeds in their lawns. None whatsoever. How do they do it? Nuke the lawn with chemicals that leach into the food chain and cause songbirds to fall dead out of trees? *When* do they do it? I never see them out with the Weed-Whacker. Maybe they have some sort of underground suction system, a subterranean network of pneumatic tubes that sucks the weeds out of the lawn and whisks them away to a holding tank somewhere under Indiana, where they're recycled and made into that green carpeting that some people put on their front steps.

We have weeds. We could nuke our lawn, and indeed paid a service an exorbitant tribute for a while to do just that, but then I saw some grim-faced person on TV saying something like, "What's more important to YOU, a perfect lawn or the earth your children will inherit?" which made me feel as if I had the values of a Barbie doll, so we quit.

However, there is no escaping from zealot neighbors; therefore, you—and everyone else who walks or drives by—will, come May, see me on hands and knees, out on the parkway, conveniently located next to passing traffic, with a dandelion yanker, doing it the old-fashioned way. Earth, I hope you appreciate all the work I go to for you. Neighbors, I hope you notice my stoop labor. (Of course, as soon as the traffic slows down, I will, too.)

The problem with all this effort is, of course, that there's always going to be someone who is more diligent than you and therefore makes you look bad. We have a nice spring flower bed— bulbs, which were here when we came, don't mind being ignored and make a nice show for a week or two. I was kind of proud of our little display, but then a young couple down the block moved in and *built* a flower bed. With three successive seasons of blooms. They also installed window boxes, painted their shutters an attractive dark green and constructed a dog run. (Of course, they don't have kids. I've noticed that many people with children downscale to a few evergreens.)

I don't know if there's any easy answer to this form of neighbor peer pressure, except maybe not *have* neighbors—do as one family I know did: Move to the country and live on ten secluded acres. But then maybe you'd have to act knowledgeable when Art and DeWayne down at the feed store ask you what you are planting this year. Or you could live among people noticeably more lax than yourself, the kind you read about in the paper, who keep eighty cats and have trouble letting their garbage leave the nest.

The thing is, though, I like our neighbors. They're almost all really nice. They'd never *say* anything about our hedge that once got so overgrown you could have sworn that you heard jungle noises emanating from it on a humid night. We're even invited to block parties.

No, this is a pressure I take upon myself—to fit in, to look good. But lately I've been thinking, *Maybe we're not alone in bowing to the law of the pack.* Seems like every time we cut our grass, the guy across the street gets out *his* lawnmower.

SAY YOU WANT A RESOLUTION ...

N ew Year's Days tend to be slow around our house. Probably because we've been up late the night before— either out somewhere, or just banging pots and pans with Amanda in the midnight chill—we take it easy January first. Sleep in, make a big breakfast, go for a walk. Nothing very strenuous. Maybe it's all this free time that inspires us to sit down and engage in that annual ritual of futility known as making New Year's resolutions.

Seems silly in a way, like the Cubs taking the field on Opening Day—you just *know* the grim outcome, so why even bother to suit up? But there we are, first thing in the morning, sitting with our yellow pad and pen. He makes resolutions. I make resolutions. We make resolutions together. Real, specific, impossible-to-achieve, sweeping goals: Be a perfect father! Be a perfect mother! Bring our bodies into complete pH balance! Read aloud to each other from the writings of the early church fathers every day! Run up and down the basement steps thirty times a week until the muscles in our eyeballs start fluttering! Plant a tree! Make a friend! Clean the condenser coils on our refrigerator regularly! Figure out where the condenser coils are!

That sort of thing. We even agree to secret the resolutions

in a safe place where they'll be undisturbed, such as in our VCR manual on the page where it tells you how to program your machine. Now that I think about it, there must be crumbling New Year's resolutions hidden all over our house—in the ironing pile, in the *Easy Crafts for a Rainy Day* book I once received from someone who didn't know me very well, in the lockbox we keep meaning to put our important papers in. Someday when we move, we will discover these records of good intentions and sigh to each other, "How young we were!"

You, of course, know the rest. For a few days we're busily engaged in useful, happy enterprise, humming as we go about our daily round, brimming with accomplishment, actually doing what we said we would do. Then, somewhere between Elvis's and Martin Luther King's birthdays, sloth begins to creep back in. We forget to record a check. We eat a Dorito. We go, "Oh, why don't we just skip Origen and rent a Bill Murray video?"

Of course, we feel guilty about this slippage. Resolutions have a purpose. They give us an ideal to strive for, help us articulate goals. On the other hand, it's no fun chasing after an ideal that keeps receding in the distance. Imagine driving on the interstate around suppertime with a carful of hungry kids and seeing the golden arches on the horizon—but as you approach, the golden arches are always just a few miles farther down the road. Beckoning. Taunting.

It's nice to achieve something, to reach a destination. Maybe, then, we just need to lower our sights a bit and make resolutions we actually can keep. Here, then, are our goals for THIS year (I have asked my accountability group, consisting of my mother, to make sure we hold to them). You may even wish to cut these out and try them yourself. After all, what's life without a challenge? The resolutions:

* Get up in the morning.
* Eat.

* Postpone at least one thing a month.
* Close the door behind you.
* Complain about the president.
* Take a shower.
* Remember to pick up milk and TP on your way home.
* Look at the time.
* Pet a dog.
* Don't get your tires rotated.
* Throw something away.
* Blink.
* Swat a mosquito.
* Avoid something unpleasant.
* Hug a member of your immediate family.
* Feel happy about God, and the fact that he'll like you
even if you botch your resolutions.

There are many more such worthy goals we can set for
ourselves, but these will do for now. As you can see, my plate's
pretty full, so I'd better go find a place to conceal this significant
document. (I think there's a space behind the condenser coils.)

ONE, TWO, THREE, HIKE!

I pirouetted in front of my husband. "How do I look?" I asked, knowing that it was safe to inquire.

His eyes told the story. "You look lovely," he said.

I had to go out of town on business, just for a day. I don't do this very often, so I wanted to look good. *Finished* good, if you know what I mean. Usually when I get dressed up there's one thing slightly off—I have a run in the foot of my stocking, or my nails aren't polished, or I'm not wearing perfume.

This time was different. I had run around the day before buying a dress (Liz Claiborne, fifty-percent markdown), shoes, hose, makeup. You should have seen me standing for an eternity in front of the drugstore cosmetics display, studying shades of blush—am I the coral type, peach, plum? Terra cotta? Hypoallergenic? Moisturizing? What can I buy that won't make me look like I've burst blood vessels in my cheeks? (Erring on the side of caution, I got a really pale pink that must have been created for albinos. It made my cheeks look whiter than the rest of my face so that I resembled a strange photo negative.)

So here I was, early in the morning, waiting for my limo. I had sewed a button on my coat. My nails were manicured. I was not wearing the white blusher. My lingerie wouldn't embarrass my mother if there were a plane crash. My hair was at that nice stage midway between "I just got a haircut" and "I MUST get a haircut." I had even cleaned my clutch bag. Lookin' good, kiddo! When the limo arrived, I quietly said good-bye to a sleeping Amanda, kissed my husband, and left my workaday world behind. I could almost hear the airline commercial music echoing in my ears.

At the airport I had some time, so I bought a cup of coffee and a copy of *TIME* and sat down at the departure gate. When the flight was called, I stood. And felt my pantyhose start to inch down.

Oh, no.

I hurried onto the plane and sat down. Maybe it was just a momentary slip. Under the guise of fastening my seatbelt, I covertly tugged. There. That should do it.

When I arrived at my destination, I was greeted by my host. *Welcome to our fair city! How was the flight? Good to see you again. We're parked right out front.* As we walked through the airport (thankfully, not a long walk), I could feel my hose heading south with every footfall. Step, slip. Step, slip. Maybe I could duck into a ladies' room before I had to meet people.

I knew it. I knew I shouldn't have worn those slick panties. I knew the stockings were a size too large. If I didn't act soon, they'd be around my knees.

At the office I waited for my host to say, "Perhaps you'd like to freshen up." He did not but talked on about all the people we were going to meet and the business that had to be transacted. I nodded and smiled and desperately looked for a hidden corner where I could surreptitiously yank. Maybe I could distract him by pretending to have a coughing fit and while he was getting me a glass of water I could dart behind a potted plant.

Providentially he said, "Let me go tell the others that you're here." "Fine!" I agreed. Hike! Whew. That should hold 'em for a while, as I had pulled the waistband halfway up my ribcage.

I was okay most of the day. The one dicey moment came

when I was taken on a tour of the building. It was a big building; therefore, I had to do lots of walking. Lots of inching. I dropped back behind my guide, who was giving the tour spiel and didn't notice, and did the deed.

Wouldn't you know? Isn't it always the way?

You spend your whole life from about age thirteen on trying to pull yourself together, and you think that maybe after thirty years and many missteps you're finally getting it right. You know what looks good on you and what doesn't. You know how to talk in front of a group without wearing a bag over your head. You remember to pop a Certs before church.

Then this—hiding like a hunted animal, jerking on your discount-store pantyhose.

I suspected it before, but now I know God has a sense of humor. He must. While I was sashaying around, so proud in my designer clothes, He was chuckling to Himself, saying, "You think you're a vision of loveliness, and so you are. But just to be sure you remember who can take the credit for that, just to keep you a little off-balance, I'll have a little fun with you."

And God's laughter is infectious. Looking back, it was sort of funny. But I'm here to tell you I shall *never* wear those slick underpants again. Give me cotton any day.

HOME SWEET HOTEL

I turned and waved at my husband. "Good-bye, Sweetie!" I called as I stepped into the jetway. "Have a good time with Amanda!"

I should have added, "I'll miss you," but I did not because it would not have been true. I was looking forward to going away for a couple of days. On an airplane. To a hotel. All by myself.

I settled into my seat, buckled myself in, looked out the window. This time my stockings were staying up. I made certain of that. And I sighed contentedly. *Alone at last.*

My family are hearts of my heart, the dearest people in the world, but I'm hardly ever alone. Or I'm alone with the bill box and the guy who keeps calling trying to sell us light bulbs and dishtowels. My house drones away at me: Do me. Do me. Once I had the bright idea of saving money by staying home for our vacation. Get away, right in your own backyard! We thought we would go to the museum, go to the zoo, have picnics, and spend vast quantities of quality time together as a family. Unfortunately, we had to come home every night. And make dinner. And answer the phone. And make the beds the next morning.

Not a particularly re-creating experience.

Sometimes you just have to escape your life for a time. That's all there is to it. All right, I wasn't exactly escaping my life;

this was business. And I've been enjoying my life recently (always a startling realization, like "How did *that* happen? Is this *me*, the world-class malcontent?"). Whatever, I was determined to enjoy it.

You don't realize how many demands you have, especially as a wife and mother, until you are physically removed from those demands. I liked the feeling of anonymity on the airplane. The nice, highly tanned steward with a professional smile and the Texas accent (people in the airline business all have Texas accents) gave me a soft drink and some peanuts. To him I was just the passenger in row 16. I liked that. He could think anything he wanted to about me—that I was some hotshot woman CEO—a visiting poet from Ireland—anything. He did not want anything from me, and that felt nice.

I probably sound as if I have a decided lack of entertainment in my life. People travel all the time and get sick of it, the in-and-out of airports, the faceless hotel rooms, the bad food, the fatigue. But, like I've said, I *don't* travel all the time. Get me in an airport and I'm kind of *Gee-whiz, this is great*, I feel part of the throbbing pulse of the global economy, fed by the arteries of the airways!

Then there was the hotel room.

My hosts led me to my room. *My* room. I turned the key, and there it was—a queen-size bed, a big-screen TV, a spotless bathroom, a view of a lake. None of the comforts of home.

This is another thing. I love hotels. Remember the Eloise books? Eloise was a rich little girl who lived at the Plaza Hotel in New York along with her nanny. When I was a kid, I thought that seemed like the height of happiness, living in a hotel. My husband and I spent our first weekend as a couple at one of Chicago's finest establishments. Fancy downtown hotels, faceless motels out by the interstate, whatever—I love the privacy, the smell of institutional cleaning supplies and flame-retardant carpet, those little shampoos and lotions they put in the bathrooms, the pads of paper. I like it when you can put the room-service card out on your door the night before and some mysterious person sees it and the next morning there's a knock on your door and presto! a little pot of coffee and maybe a muffin, just for you to savor along with the complimentary newspaper.

I don't want to go to some bed-and-breakfast, where the hostess knows my name and I have to interact with the other guests. I want to be left alone, and I don't care about ambiance. Once my husband was interviewing for a job in a New Hampshire village in the heart of leaf-peeper country and took Amanda, still a nursing infant, and me along. We stayed at a quaint inn, and they put us up in a room the size of a walk-in closet. There was barely enough room for the portacrib. We literally had to go into the bathroom to get dressed. Worse, the room was above the lounge, so we were kept awake much of the night by the strains of "Proud Mary" and "Stayin' Alive" thumping away below. The next day we were all exhausted; my husband did not get the job (which in retrospect was a sign of God's providence, because shortly thereafter the New England economy went down the tubes), and we drove to Boston, hating quaintness. There we stayed at a huge high-rise Hilton near the Mass Pike, with no view, no ambiance, but the room was big and quiet, and we all slept for hours.

I did the same thing when I arrived at my hotel. Then I awoke, looked around and thought, *Hmmm, still have a little time before dinner. What shall I do now?* I wandered out onto the balcony and looked at the geese and ducks for a few minutes. I clicked the TV remote and dialed through cable channels. (We don't get cable. Had the basic package for a while as a free trial, but I could never figure out how to find the Disney channel, the only thing we were really interested in. I always kept landing on someone selling jewelry or some Spanish-language variety show.) I opened the desk drawer to see if there was any stationery. Had a great time.

Here is what would be ideal from my point of view: two

or three days away, at a hotel, every month. Maybe by myself, maybe with a couple of girlfriends but not sharing a room. The room is *mine*. Just enough time to recharge the batteries, enough time to watch a movie on TV from start to finish, preferably something unutterably sad and chastely romantic, like that movie with Cary Grant and Deborah Kerr where he's supposed to meet her at the Empire State Building and she doesn't show up and then he finds out she was in an accident. I can still remember the music.

Interestingly, I don't think my husband feels the same need. He escapes by getting in the car and driving by himself. He likes being able to play his tapes without some kid saying, "Daddy, that's too loud!" He likes to drink coffee without some nagging female complaining about spilling, and turn left against oncoming traffic without some nagging female shrieking, "Look out for that hazardous-materials truck bearing down!"

Back to the weekend. Everything went pretty well, I got to fly one more time, and as the plane taxied to the gate I saw my family watching through the window. I waved like crazy at them, they saw me and waved back, Amanda jumping up and down with excitement, and we had a joyful reunion.

Then I studied my daughter. Her hair was stringy, she looked vaguely ill-clad, and there was chocolate around her mouth. "You didn't give her her bath, did you?" I asked my husband. Well, no. She didn't feel like taking one. What did you have for dinner? Pizza. What's this chocolate from? Well, you see, we were at the store and she wanted some cookies, and since you were gone I . . .

Here I imagined my daughter pining away for me; but apparently Mom isn't the only one who has a good time when she goes away. There's more than one way to escape from each other.

We talked all the way home, filling each other in. Eager to counteract sugar overload in my child, I gave Amanda an apple from my complimentary fruit basket. My husband and I smiled at each other. "It's good to have you home," he said. "That bed gets lonesome." Once when he was changing lanes I shouted, "Watch out! Car in your blind spot!"

Ah, there's nothing like familiarity.

BEWARE OF THE
BROKEN GLASS

Yesterday Fritz was reaching for something deep in the kitchen cupboard and inadvertently knocked over the flour canister. I didn't think it would break, but it did. It shattered all over the kitchen floor. Oh, well, accidents happen. Fritz swept up the glass and tried to save as much of the flour as he could. Why waste it? The floor was clean. Well, relatively.

I didn't think any more about the incident until I decided to bake some bread. Fritz sifted and strained the flour to make sure there were no grains of glass still hiding therein. Contentedly I went about mixing up and licking the batter. An hour later two golden loaves emerged from the oven, fragrant with nutmeg, flaky-textured with shortening.

We sat down to eat. Fritz cut himself a hefty slice and eagerly bit into it—and made a face. "Glass!" he said.

I cautiously tore off a chunk. Seemed okay. Tasted great. I can leave candy and pastries alone, but boy, do I love a good bread. I could easily stand in the kitchen with no one looking, slicing off little pieces "just to even it out," until half the loaf has disappeared and I suddenly have this mental picture of what I must look like, furtively stuffing . . .

I took another bite and felt something crunch. It wasn't the crust.

Suffice it to say, it was a long dinner. Tearing off little pieces of bread, inspecting them for bits of mica, taking tiny nibbles. We did not want to throw away the bread because, as I said, it was really good and we were to that point every family comes to when you're so low on food you resort to using those olives that have been in your refrigerator for months and wonder if they count as a vegetable. Still, though, as I swallowed the bread, I had visions of my esophagus being cut to ribbons by invisible glass. Amanda, sensibly, shunned the bread in favor of saltines but watched in fascination as Mom and Dad risked their digestive tracts with every bite.

"I don't understand," I said to Fritz as he tore and inspected. "I thought we got all that glass out. I thought we'd been really thorough."

"Doesn't take much," he said, discreetly using his napkin.

I thought about this later as I was cleaning up the kitchen and trying not to even out the bread. Sharp, nasty glass. Wholesome, nourishing bread, the staff of life. What can we learn from this, class, aside from *Don't put off grocery shopping so long that you'll stoop to eating anything, no matter how questionable?*

Just this: You can't be too careful.

I've got all these tiny shards of bad things in my life I have to keep sifting out. It's when I think I've gotten rid of them all that I get cocky and complacent, and then *crunch*! I speak too sharply to my child, or husband, or I disappoint a friend or spend too much time dwelling on myself. So I have to keep inspecting my life for these infinitesimal pieces of danger.

Yet I'm never going to get all the pieces. The glass that found its way into our bread was almost microscopic; we could have sifted and strained and inspected for hours and it still would not have been enough. I can't root out every sin, every misstep.

Not by myself. And I don't have to, thank God. That's a comforting feeling—even more comforting than the taste of a big, yeasty slice of hot bread, straight from the oven, smeared with real butter . . .

Which reminds me. We've about finished up the nutmeg bread. I'd make some more, but I think we're out of flour.

E.T., THE TOOTH FAIRY,
AND THE CRY
IN THE NIGHT

*M*om—mee!"

"What?"

"C'mere."

"Just a minute."

"C'mere."

Sigh. "I'm in the bathroom!"

"Come *now*!"

So I hurriedly finish up and go now because, of course, mothers are not bound by the physical laws that other mortals are subject to. She wants a graham cracker. She is perfectly capable of getting one for herself, but somehow it tastes better when purveyed by Mom.

Or I am working.

"MOM!"

"What?" I call, trying to keep from sounding irritated. I have got to get this project done and in the mail. Just one more paragraph should do it.

"I hurt myself."

I want to yell back, "You're not hurt unless you're unconscious, immobile, or hemorrhaging," but I do not.

"Come NOW!"

I bang myself on the corner of the desk and trip over a pile of papers as I rush to her side. "What is it?"

"I dropped my dolly on my foot, and it doesn't feel good."

I make a show of inspecting for bruises and kiss the injured member. Meanwhile, I am certain I'm developing a hematoma on my hip where I hit myself. "There. You're fine."

Or I have put her to bed, early for a change. Now I have some time for myself. I am just settling down to read the magazine that came in the mail a month ago, one of the many inviting selections in my dust-covered "To Read" basket, when I hear a plaintive "Ma!"

Ma goes.

"I'm afraid E.T. is going to spy into the window."

"Honey. The shades are drawn tight. E.T. is not real. Your night light is on. And remember, Jesus is watching over you."

"Can Jesus see me?"

"He sure can."

"Does He know I lost a tooth?"

"Yep."

"Is Jesus the tooth fairy?"

Oh, dear. This is not the time for a teachable moment. "No, He is not."

"But you always say Jesus can do anything."

"He can. Now go to sleep!"

It has been this way since she was born. First she cried for me from her crib, and I went—usually a couple of times a night. I never *didn't* go. Now, even though she is reading chapter books and shooting out of her clothes, even though she is growing up with a dizzying speed, she still calls for me. There are times when only Mom will do. She calls for me, and it never occurs to her that

I won't come. Because I always do come. I always come because there will come a day when she'll be tucking herself into bed, when instead of calling out for me she'll call her friends on the phone. I'll be able to finish reading that magazine. No one will interrupt me when I'm working. I may even be early in meeting my deadlines.

Maybe I'm too easy on her. Maybe she needs to be taught that moms have lives, too. But I guess I would rather teach her trust. Because if I am available and interruptible, if she knows she can always count on me, maybe I can, in some small way, show her—and not just tell her—a little of the way that God loves her and cares about even the smallest concerns.

I reminded myself of Amanda just a few nights ago. I was printing something out at church from a floppy disk. I finished running the file and someone came into the office. Distracted, I removed the disk and placed it . . . somewhere.

When I went to gather up my work, I couldn't find the disk.

I looked everywhere: in the wastebasket, under the computer, inside the laser printer. The thing had simply gotten up and walked away. Tears of frustration filled my eyes. I had to have it because it contained almost an entire book, and I didn't have copies of all the chapters.

I prayed quickly, "Lord, you know my needs. Please, let that disk be found." It probably sounds shallow and inconsequential, the wrong thing to pray for, perhaps, but doesn't the Bible say, "Cast your cares on Him"? This was a care. Just like the way that Amanda turns to me when she sustains even the most minor injury, I turned to God—and I assumed that He would come to the rescue.

The church secretary found the disk later that evening. Somehow it had gotten lodged in a crack under the A drive. The secretary said, "I went to put my own disk in and it just popped out!"

Thank you, God, I thought.

Was it childlike to think that God had caused that disk to be found? Immature to posit some relationship between prayers and results? Doesn't God have better things to do than worry about some woman looking for a five-and-a-quarter-inch piece of magnetic plastic? Wasn't it all my fault because I didn't copy my file? Wasn't the *real* lesson "always run a backup"?

No more than the real lesson to Amanda is: "Be more careful when you're playing, because your mother doesn't want to be interrupted when you're hurt."

I don't always want to be interrupted. Sometimes I go to my child grudgingly. And there's the difference: God *wants* us to call on Him. This Father, who laid the foundations of the universe, is never too busy to attend to His children.

There's another difference. Amanda won't always call for me in the night, because she won't always be there in the night. But God's nest is never empty. I'll always be there to interrupt. And I hope I can teach Amanda to call on her Father, too. He can do ever so much more than that silly tooth fairy who stumbles into her room around midnight and sticks loose change under her pillow.

CRUMBS UNDER THE BED, AND A LESSON

We sat on the floor, Amanda and I.

We were in a patch of sun on her carpet. The door to her room was closed. The lovely young thing who does our cleaning was bumping the vacuum against it.

We try to do this every Saturday: to make some time when she sits in my lap and we talk quietly. No playmates around, no TV, no work, or school, or fatigue. This time we were sequestered in her room, snuggling on the floor.

We talked.

"Mom, is God magic?"

"Well, I don't know if 'magic' is the right word. God is all-powerful, though."

"Could God make me fly?" Amanda has tried to fly periodically ever since she was about three.

"I suppose if He wanted to He could. But God made you so you can't fly, so He must not want you to fly. He always has His reasons."

"When I get to heaven, maybe then I'll be able to fly, because you always say that in heaven everything will be perfect."

Something very cold got me in its grip, the icy, secret fear that lies buried way down in all parents, the fear that drives us to check on our children night after night and greet them jubilantly in the morning. *When I get to heaven* ...

No.

I held Amanda close, saying nothing, near tears, overwhelmed with my love for this little girl, this fierce, strong mother-love that is like no other feeling in the world. Gradually the icy fear ebbed away. "Amanda," I said after a time.

"What?"

"Stay here always. Never go away."

"I won't. I'll never get married. I'll live with you and Daddy forever."

Of course that's not what must be. What must be is that she goes away, probably gets married, maybe moves halfway across the country. Away from me. I have known children who never left, grew old with Mom and Dad. Fifty-year-old kids living with eighty-year-old parents, a terrible distortion of what God intends. I don't want that. I want grandchildren, a place to go visit, carrying a carpetbag full of toys and Lifesavers for the little ones. "Grandma's here!"

But just because it must be, doesn't mean I have to like it.

"They'll be gone before you know it," I'm told. One day they're taking their first steps. The next, bang! they're asking you for the car keys. Like Emily out in the other room, bumping the vacuum around.

Do I appreciate my child enough, right now, while she *is* with me? Am I too quick to say, "I can't come now, I have to finish this paragraph," or "Please, find something else to do—this house is a mess and I can't talk"?

I wonder.

When was the last time I said, "Amanda, would you like to play with me right now? Amanda, let's go for a walk"? Do I say, often enough, "You know, you're a good kid"?

I tightened my arms around her. She snuggled, as she has since she was a newborn. The nurse in the hospital, carrying Amanda in to me to be nursed, said, "A lot of newborns squirm when you hold them. She's such a cuddler, we all want to take her home with us." What a gift I hold in my arms right now. What a precious gift. Lord, I am not worthy.

The patch of sun moved across the carpeting. Finally I had to get up; Emily had to come in and vacuum. Good thing, too — from my vantage point on the floor I could see crumbs hiding under the bed.

I gave Amanda a final squeeze, and we stood up. I decided not to say anything about the crumbs.

THE FAMILY WHO FELL
OFF THE CHARTS

O ne day my husband was dialing around on the radio,
looking for something to listen to. He finally settled on
one of those stations that plays syrupy love songs from the
seventies. Barry Manilow, Neil Diamond, Lionel Ritchie . . . you
know the type. "Not that," I said. "It's not for us. That's for
twenty-eight-year-old single white women who work in suburban
office complexes."

"Well, what is for us?"

I got in the shower and pondered the question. What *is*
for us? Not the contemporary Christian station. That's for the
college kids. Not the traditional Christian station, the one with the
preachers and the Haven of Rest Quartet. That's for their
grandmothers. The classic rock station? Nope; when I listen to it I
always feel slightly embarrassed and silly, like I don't want anyone
to know I sing along with "Stairway to Heaven." Talk radio? That
seems to be aimed at some weird subset of socially isolated
individuals who are FED UP and AREN'T GOING TO TAKE IT
ANYMORE. I imagine their cleaning their high-powered rifles
before getting on the horn to unleash their bile on the talk-show
host.

"Maybe the public radio station," I called out to him. "The quirky, eclectic one that plays everything from bluegrass to tuneless jazz that goes on and on." That's us, out on the fringe of the FM band.

This always happens to us. We never fit into any category someone else has devised. We are demographic anomalies.

I once read a book where the author tried to define about twenty or so socio-cultural-economic categories in America. He had broken them down into groups ranging down the scale from "Country Clubs, Topsiders, and Martoonis" to "Shotguns, Pickup Trucks, and Real Mean Dogs," or something like that. There were categories for *everything*—liberals who live in city high-rises with hidden cameras in the lobbies and buy ugly modern art; wealthy suburban housewives who drive Volvo station wagons; small-businesspersons who vote Republican and live in greater Thief River Falls, Minnesota. I think he even included the homeless.

But he didn't include us. I can't remember now, but it may have even had a "Where Do *You* Fit In?" sort of self-diagnostic. I looked for us, and we were missing. The guy didn't have a category for Poor-But-Well-Educated Christian Professionals Living in a Highly Taxed Outer Suburban Area.

We're not blue collar. We're not wealthy. We *are* WASPs. If you looked at the way we grew up, we should be nominal Episcopalians. We are not; we're solid, low-church, pietistic evangelicals. We live in a college town, and we own a lot of books, but we're not academics. We're not a young family, but we have a young child. We don't fit.

I think I know the answer. Market researchers, the people for whom such categorizing nonsense is written, hate us, and therefore we have been deleted from their computer models. They hate us because we are essentially nonconsumers who have no intention of purchasing whatever they're pushing.

Every now and then we'll get a phone call from some

researcher, asking about our buying habits. "Have you been in a department store in the last month?" No. "Are you planning to take an airplane trip in the next six months?" Yes, but only because someone else is paying for it. "Have you purchased any major appliances in the past year?" I don't know. Does the electric hair cutter that my husband got a great deal on at a garage sale count? No? "Are you familiar with any of the top-ten-rated TV shows?" Sorry, we're not. Ask me about *Beauty and the Beast*. I do a great imitation of Gaston.

The survey person always sounds patient and somewhat perplexed, almost as if she does not know how to communicate with us. Like we're that tribe in the Philippines that some guy found and thought was out of the Stone Age (only later it turned out that they lived in a trailer park outside Manila and were pulling this scam and just wanted the rights for a made-for-TV movie, with the requirement that Dennis Weaver play the idealistic, overly credulous white guy).

We hardly ever buy anything beyond the basics of food, toilet paper, hair-thickening shampoo for my husband . . . things like that. Home office supplies, sometimes, but that's a business expense. We buy secondhand cars every two or three years. Lawn fertilizer maybe once a year. When we *do* make a major purchase, which we do only when something breaks down and/or when we have determined that the item is not available at a garage sale or as a castoff from a church friend, we walk into the retailer and gaze around all wide-eyed, thinking, *So this is a department store.* Kind of like Robin Williams as the Russian guy in *Moscow on the Hudson* when he went into Bloomingdale's and asked for "blue gins."

We recently engaged a couple of financial planners to help us figure out what to do with our vast holdings, and in preparation sat down and filled out a financial profile. When we came to the "Discretionary Expenses" category, we had to rack our brains. Recreation? Entertainment? "Let's see, we get Amanda a Happy

Meal every now and then," I mused. "I guess that counts. Okay, I'll put down ten dollars a month for entertainment."

I'm not exactly certain how this state of nonconsumption came about. Part of it is due to the fact that our periodic poverty has at times limited our consumption options. Part of it is philosophical. (Try explaining the parable of the rich fool to some market researcher. She won't get it.) And part of it may be a residue of our countercultural youth, a secret delight in beating the system by doing things like buying a dishwasher for twenty-five dollars from a guy who had it out in his driveway with a "FOR SALE" sign on it.

So here we are, the Midwestern equivalent of some undiscovered tribe that time forgot. According to the researchers, we don't exist. (I wonder if the IRS has found out about our nonexistence yet. I should let them know.)

But I forgot. There is one area of conspicuous consumption that I neglected to mention. All I have to do is go into Amanda's bedroom and look at the dolls lining her shelves. There's All-American Barbie, Rollerblading Barbie, Heavy-Metal Barbie, Driven-Lady-Lawyer Barbie, Physically Challenged Barbie . . . you name it, we've spent money on it. I know the layout of the toy department at Venture almost as well as I know the smile lines on my dear mother's face. My kid has so many dolls I could almost list them as dependents on our tax return.

Well, you can't be totally rigid in your anticonsumption ideology, can you? Why deprive your innocent child? Admittedly some of them were given to her. But not all, not all. So maybe we do exist after all. I wonder if the sociographics people have a category for Sucker Parents.

MOM'S SECOND CHILDHOOD

*A*manda shoves a bag in my face. "Smell."

I sniff—and am instantly transported to golden summers of the past. "Fizzies!" I crow. There's no mistaking that violently grapey scent. Of course she's not drinking Fizzies. She's eating Fruit Snacks, purchased for her by her benevolent, all-loving father when they went to the market. Fruit Snacks, for the uninitiated, are these rubbery little confections that come in what are ostensibly fruit flavors but bear as much resemblance to real grapes, lemons, and oranges as a Kingdom Hall bears to St. John the Divine Cathedral. As they say, kids love 'em.

I give my husband a look. "Well, it's fruit," he says lamely.

She has her Fruit Snacks. I had my Fizzies, those neat little tablets that you'd drop in water and they would fizz and make a highly sweetened, utterly-without-redeeming-nutritional-value drink. Every generation has its junk food. I remember reading in a book (it might have been E. B. White's *Stuart Little*) about something called "sarsaparilla." I thought it sounded delicious, maybe something like peach nectar, until I learned that it's brown and made from some awful root.

One of the interesting discoveries about having children is

how you're able to relive parts of your childhood through them. I smell the ersatz fruit and I'm a sweaty kid in shorts and a sleeveless blouse, drinking Fizzies on a hot August afternoon. Fake fruit smells are a great way to recapture those halcyon days. The odor of calamine lotion does that for me, too. Suddenly I'm seven years old and lying in bed writhing from chickenpox itch while my mother smears that pink goo on the poxes.

Beverly Cleary books, new sneakers, lemonade stands, the thrill of Christmas morning, winning the spelling championship in sixth grade, jumping in leaf piles ... it all comes back. Ah, childhood.

Other sights and sounds and smells come crowding in, too. Memories such as ...

Sitting on the cold wooden gym floor in fourth grade, wearing my blue gymsuit. The captains are picking teams for dodgeball. Watching as first the brawny, athletic girls get chosen, then the tiny gymnastics types, then the average girls, then finally it's me and several other castoffs, one of whom has a discernible lack of large motor skills.

Bursting into tears at my birthday party the year I turned five because (a) my mother would not let me wear Mary Janes like the other girls; (b) I hardly knew the other kids, since they were assorted children of my parents' friends; and (c) my grandmother had given me a shiny red scooter and I could not figure out how to ride it properly. I think I sulked the whole time, just like Amanda's fictional favorite, Ramona Quimby.

Measles. Mumps. German measles. Tonsillitis. Strep throat. Scarlet fever. Delirium. Choking down bitter-tasting green-and-white penicillin capsules. Having to lie in my parents' bed and watch *Art Linkletter's House Party* on their portable TV because it was too early for cartoons to come on and I felt too sick to read.

Having to dissect worms in freshman biology. Slitting the worm open and looking into the interior and being unsure what

I'm supposed to get excited about—all those little white strands? Being afraid to ask the teacher—who periodically singles me out for public exhortation—what it is I'm supposed to see and why I should care. Being afraid to ask my lab partner, a guy with a Lithuanian name and no sense of humor, who at the age of fourteen has already decided he is going to become a Nobel laureate.

Stepping on prickly cockleburs on the white sands of a Florida Gulf Coast beach when I was three. That and the fishy-sweet smell of the sea, which still returns to me on wild spring days when the wind and humidity are right, stand out. I don't remember much else—a gray-shingled general store, a causeway, a broad-eaved beachfront white house surrounded by palmetto trees—but I have the feeling if I went there now looking for it I couldn't find it.

Cringing and trying to make myself invisible as I walk past a gang of big boys, all of whom have somehow found out my last name and make fun of it.

As a matter of fact, I think I spent much of my childhood in this state of near-terror, wishing I could disappear, poof! Like when I would be doodling on my arithmetic workbook with a ballpoint pen, getting ink all over my hands, and the teacher would suddenly call on me: "Betsey, I'm sure *you* can tell us how to multiply this fraction."

Or when I would walk past a large and unchained dog who, I was certain, was semiferal and walking with an odd, jerky gait. I had heard dogs walk funny when they have rabies. Dogs ran free then, bounding over the open meadows that had not yet been bulldozed for houses with three-car garages and basement rec rooms. I remember my dad, who had a habit of making voice-of-doom pronouncements, looking out of the window and saying in an ominous tone, "I don't like it. The dogs are starting to pack." I envisioned packs of dogs with dripping fangs, reverting to the wild state, ready to prey on small children who wanted nothing more than to play archaeologist and dig up small mammal bones in the thickets. We romantically imagined they had dragged themselves there to die; now I think the bones had probably been dropped by careless owls.

Sometimes I wanted to be invisible for no reason other than I just did not want to be bothered. Life was too taxing; the fun part was watching everything, like a fly on the wall. You knew everything about them; they couldn't even see you.

The interesting thing about these memories is that they have nothing to do with my parents or anything they did or did not do. I hear people talk now about "making memories" for your kids, the idea being that if you take your children on enough trips and spend enough time with them building model rockets and going for walks and pointing out wildflowers ("Look, there's a wildflower! Haven't seen one in years!"), you'll bequeath your children a treasure of memories that will warm them in years to come.

Well, I try to do that. But if Amanda's anything like I was—like I suspect a lot of sensitive kids are—she has this whole other subterranean, secret kid life that I know nothing about and cannot really enter into without seeming sort of strange and despairing: "Amanda, are you ever in terror? Do you know you will hate biology?"

I'm supposed to be the provider of hope, of laughter, and encouragement. I can't say these things. But what I maybe *can* say is "I know how you feel." Maybe that's enough.

And I can already predict one memory of mine she'll be spared. If they ever pick teams, which I don't think they do anymore because it hurts kids' self-esteem (a term that hadn't even been invented when I was a kid, because kids weren't supposed to have selves)—if they ever pick teams, Amanda will be the one making the selections. Thank God for paternal athletic genes.

PRAYER FOR A GRAY DAY

*O*h, Lord, it's one of those days.

Gray sky, raw wind, spits of snow coming down. (Why am I telling *You* about the weather?)

I think if I look at my piles one more time I'm going to scream.

Some days it seems all I do is move pieces of paper around. Lord, I don't think they had paper clutter when You were among us. Maybe there's a lesson there.

Amanda just said, "You're crabby, Mommy."

Yes. I am. How can I tell her it's my day of the month to be crabby? To feel edgy and jumpy and ugly and unwanted? Please, Father, help me to be patient with her. It's not her fault, after all.

These work pressures have me down. Day after day I get up, go to the computer, try to write words that glorify You and help Your people. I know I'm where You would have me, and some days the words have wings. But today it feels like they're wearing leaden weights.

I think I need a vacation, Lord. How long has it been?

On top of everything, I cut my finger when I was dusting and it HURTS.

Father, You know what I'm feeling. You've felt everything I'm feeling. I don't have to tell You about hurt.

Did You ever have days like this, Lord? Days when You weren't healing the sick or preaching to the multitudes or calming the storm? In-between days? Frustrating days? I guess You did. But why is it so hard to find You on days like this, the in-between gray days?

When Dad went to be with You and I cried myself almost inside out, I knew Your arms were wrapped around me. When Amanda was born and the tears were for overflowing joy, I knew You were there in the birthing room. I feel You with me when I'm lost in the storm and when I'm skipping in the sunshine.

But this . . .

You speak through the whirlwind and the burning bush. You speak from the heavens. Do You also speak through the paper piles, the dusty desk, the laundry that needs sorting? Can I hear You through the ringing telephone, the demands of my family, the funny squeak in the car? Can I see You through overcast?

I know You're there. You've always been there for me. You sought me even before I knew You.

I guess this is where trust comes in, Lord.

Trust that You're still holding me up, even though I don't feel Your hands.

Trust that somehow I will get through this day, this dreary, more-of-the-same day. (Lord, is it okay sometimes to pray, "Father, just help me make it through this day"? We creatures set our sights low sometimes.)

Trust that I can recognize You through the overcast—in my daughter's laugh, in a small task completed, in the words of a well-loved book. Trust that You really care about that one paper pile that never seems to shrink.

Father, forgive me for my limited vision. Forgive me for

my impatience and my focus on myself. Forgive me for my complaining.

What's that? "You're human, after all," You say?

Oh.

So I am.

Then it's okay to feel like this sometimes? You don't mind if I complain to You? Who better, You say?

Thank You, Lord. I'll remember that and try not to be so hard on myself.

Wait a minute. There's the sunshine, coming through my dirty windows. The sun is breaking through!

Oh. That's right. *You* knew that.

YOU CAN STUFF, BUT
YOU CAN'T HIDE

*T*he other day I was making our queen-size bed and banged my foot on something protruding from under the bed. I kicked it, and it immediately retreated, back into that dark country whose interior no explorer has charted. Some people have dust kitties under their beds. I have an entire Papua New Guinea of unknown objects. Some people have carpeting under their beds. I have a repository of archaeological artifacts. In fact, I think they're in layers, like the eras of ancient Jerusalem. (Nobody has ever given me a lucid explanation of why that happens. Do entire cities just sort of sink over time? Did successive ancient civilizations have backhoes that pushed their predecessors into the desert sand?)

I have theories about what is under the bed. Mind you, they are only theories. But if I were to hazard a guess (and "hazard" is the operative word here), I would speculate that the geological strata include the following:

* A Thanksgiving turkey that my daughter made in kindergarten out of her hand, aluminum foil, shell macaroni, and maybe bacon bits. It did not fit in any of the drawers in which I save her school papers, and there's something in a mother that

cannot throw away a turkey made by her own daughter's hands, so it was exiled to the hinterlands. I think I've heard its pitiful gobble once or twice.

* A really ugly painting of Venice that my husband picked up at a garage sale, the kind of artwork you see on the walls of the Best Western in Sleepy Eye, Minnesota, except that ours has a broken frame.

* Some dried-up pieces of Kleenex I threw on the floor one night when I was sick with a cold and didn't want to get up and go over to the wastebasket.

* I happen to know there's a huge wrench under there. For some reason it was lying on my husband's dresser one day and I thought (honest), *We can't have this showing in the bedroom. Someone could bludgeon us with it in the night.* I would have put it on the "out to the garage" pile on the back porch, except that company came over and I stuffed it under the bed, where it reposes still.

* Crumpled Precious Moments gift wrap that probably came from the same place we got the Best Western artwork.

* An old briefcase stuffed with folders pertaining to something, I forget what.

* Socks.

* High-school yearbooks with humiliating photos of me—wearing glasses.

Those are just some of the happy permanent dwellers of the netherworld under the bed. There's also a floating population of squatters that come and go. When we have serious company, I clean. I clean for dinner guests, for my mother, for my mother-in-law—frenzied vacuuming and polishing and spraying. I even pick up when Tom the Handyman comes over. Part of this cleaning program consists of grabbing and stuffing (remember the wrench). I grab the bill box and stuff it under the bed. I grab the Sunday paper and stuff it under there. I've even been known to grab some knickknack I didn't like and hide it under the bed.

My question is, do other people do this? Or are we the only ones? I've never heard anyone talk about this, ever. There are people whose homes I've visited who have nothing *out* except furniture and a few books. Are they those disgustingly perfect people who handle a piece of paper only once and have color-coded files and a memory basket for every child? I mean, I've been in kitchens where the only objects on the counters were bowls of fruit and ceramic geese. No toaster, no microwave, no dish drainer. What'd they do, cram the microwave under the bed when company came? Or did they use the closet?

This is getting really embarrassing, but as long as I'm laying bare the contents of my life I'll continue. Our closet, for some reason, has this ledge thing on the side. Perfect for piles. Perfect for stashing that undone mending and ironing, that sweater I used to like but have now decided makes me look like Mike Singletary in full uniform. Perfect for stowing things we usually have out but deem too unsightly for the tender eyes of our guests—that spindly plant I'm trying to coax along; my husband's weights that he keeps saying he'll use and over which I keep tripping. The slippers we usually keep in a corner of the bedroom.

Please, when you come over, do not look in our desk drawers, under the bathroom sink (I wanted to get an old-fashioned pedestal sink to replace our vanity, but my husband said, "Where would we put our junk?" "Good point," I agreed), in the basement (it isn't navigable), or in our kitchen cabinets. I have friends who are casual, unparanoid hostesses. If I want, say, a cup of coffee, they say: "Help yourself; the mugs are in the cabinet next to the refrigerator." However, at my house, if someone says, "Where do you keep the sugar?" I jump up and hastily say, "Don't worry! I'll get it for you! You go sit down and relax!"

We haven't even started on the garage or the basement.

I've been known to hide entire pieces of furniture—"Fritz, take that easy chair down to the basement, it has a stain on it." "But where will people sit?" "Who cares? They can sit in that ramrod-straight ornamental antique chair meant for eighteenth-century bodies. Out!"

The problem with all this grabbing and stuffing is, of course, that sometimes we forget what we've hidden until months later, when we stumble upon something: "Look! Here's that Joke-a-Day calendar we were going to give to Uncle Mitch for Christmas! What's it doing under the kitchen sink?" I've banished so much furniture to the basement over the years that I'm starting to fear that our entire foundation will sink down to bedrock, taking our house with it. Then we really WILL be an archaeological layer, with only a mysterious grassy mound at Webster and Forest as a reminder to future generations that once a civilization lived and loved and stowed here.

I keep thinking the day will come when we'll be clean through and through, when I can let guests rifle my kitchen cupboards, when I can go, "Here, let's hang up your coats in our closet." I even wonder if I'll ever plumb the unexplored depths Under the Bed, like a domestic Jacques Cousteau, and bring its murky contents, including the scorned turkey, up to the sunshine and fresh air once again.

Well, it's easy enough to get rid of junk. It'd even be easy enough to stop worrying about what people think and leave out the worn old moccasins and telltale bill box. Sometimes, though—especially after a day when I've scolded my daughter and been generally hard to live with—I have a sneaky feeling that I'd be a lot better off worrying not about what everyone thinks but what *Someone* thinks. Maybe I can stuff, but I can't hide. Not really.

And there's a relief in that, to tell the truth. Keeping up appearances gets exhausting after a while. That wrench must weigh ten pounds.

GIFT FROM A STRANGER

Y ou never know how God is going to use you.

I was speaking at a women's retreat in Indiana. I had come to talk to this group about friendships in the church, about loneliness and dropping the masks and reaching out to one another. And I was scared.

The first evening was fun. We all laughed as one young mom put on a skit about attempting to have a quiet time while the baby napped. We had all been there. Later we watched as one of the women got treated to a beauty makeover and color analysis, and I learned that I had been doing everything all wrong all these years, that I should NEVER wear navy because it "drains my face," and my skin was probably silently crying out for help under the punishment I was giving it.

The next morning I got up, went through my inadequate, cursory skin and makeup routine, dressed, ate, relished being by myself. Then the thing I was about to do hit me. *Lord*, I prayed. *Who am I that I should stand before these women and impart wisdom? Use me, Lord. Use me. Not my message but Yours. So many speakers. So many words. So much we've all heard before. In one ear and out the other. God, it's over to You. She who has ears to hear . . .*

I guess the talk went well; I never know how to gauge these things. I told some stories about myself, admitted my shyness, made them laugh. Entertaining talk, now let's move along to lunch.

What is really amazing is what happened after lunch.

We broke into small groups and shared prayer requests that had been written on cards. One woman wrote anonymously. She had been going to the church for four years, she wrote, and still felt as if she didn't know anyone well. She struggled with loneliness. She asked for prayers that she might be able to reach out to someone, and that person to her.

I did not cry, but I wanted to. I felt shaken and awed by her admission—and by the realization that my words (or God's) might have played some small part in helping her reveal herself.

Dear woman, I thought. *Dear, brave woman to reveal yourself like this. I don't know what it cost you to be this open, even under the cloak of anonymity.* I wanted to hug her, tell her she was loved, tell her there were people out there who wanted to be her friend. I wanted to tell her I was glad she had had the courage to come to this weekend, feeling lonely in a crowd as she did. (As we *all* have at one time or another.) I glanced around, wondering which woman she was. That pretty, twenty-something young person over there? The lady who laughed so appreciatively during my talk? That sweet-faced older woman? Who?

I'll never know, and it's not given me to know. But now, back home, back to the reality of making my own bed and getting my own coffee, I think of her, and I want her to know what a precious gift she gave me, me just happy to get away for a couple of days, me praying that in some small way I might have an impact.

Apparently, I did.

As scared as I get, as inadequate as I sometimes feel, I do like to speak. I like making people laugh. I like to get away from the routine; I enjoy meeting new people and thinking about something and someone beyond my own concerns. It's nice having others beyond my own circle to pray for.

But I don't have to go away to hotel food and confusing shower faucets to be used by God. I can do it right here, even in my own family. All I have to do is ask him: *Please, Lord, use me. Use me at home. Use me with my friends. Use me in my marriage. Use me as a mom.*

And He will, sometimes in the most surprising ways.

Thanks, Indiana friend. I will never forget what you've done for me. I feel a little less alone now, and I hope you do, too.

MY ESCAPE FROM FASHION

R emember the passages in Deuteronomy where God, in
graphic detail, tells the Israelites of the curses He will rain
upon them if they disobey His commands? He warns that those
who do not follow the Lord's commands will be afflicted with
incurable boils, dire poverty, madness . . . just for starters. Several
times God repeats, "You will become a thing of horror."

A thing of horror. This description occurred to me this
morning when I went out to take Amanda to school. I was running
late, so I quickly showered, pulled on the same skirt I had worn
the day before, didn't bother with makeup, and jammed a wool
hat—kind of a beanie—over my wet hair. It was cold outside, so
my wet hair froze into icy sticks that hung down from under my
hat and into my seemingly lashless eyes. I think I had a scratch on
my chin. I probably looked, well—peculiar. And the thing was
that I didn't care. I even laughed to myself about my appearance. I
wasn't going to be seeing anybody. Amanda likes me however I
look. The other children we were driving hardly noticed; to them
I'm just an ancient mom and maybe a slightly eccentric one at that.

I really must be getting old. There was a time I would not
have set foot outside the house even to pick up the newspaper or
bring in the empty garbage cans without at least powdering my
nose and combing my hair. As someone once said, the only time I

was without mascara was on the delivery table—and that only because sweat and tears obliterated it.

Time was I just had to have a different outfit for every day of the week. What would people think? Time was I tried to keep up with fashion. In the sixties I wore dents in my head sleeping on huge rollers. In the seventies I tottered around on platform shoes. In the eighties I attempted to look serious in thick-shouldered jackets.

I just don't bother anymore. Didn't Franklin Roosevelt enunciate four freedoms? Freedom from want, freedom from fear, and so on. I've added a fifth: Freedom from fashion. I have adopted a classic style (meaning I rotate about three or four outfits, day after day, week after week). I shop about twice a year. I've finally made my peace with my naturally curly hair, the fact that I can never have a long, silky mane like the models. (Once my dear spouse looked at me appraisingly and said, "You know, your hair looks a little like Bill Clinton's." We tell each other everything.)

Now I look, well, comfortable. Okay, sometimes I look good, like the time I took the business trip, but currently I'm not trying so hard, and it's a relief. I used to read the magazines and think, *I'm doing everything I'm supposed to be doing and somehow I still don't look like these pictures.* I used to waste money on clothes I'd wear once and then would capriciously decide looked wrong for me. It all got to be too much effort. And really, didn't Jesus say something about not worrying about what we wear?

If this is what it means to get old, I think I can live with it. Maybe I'm even getting old enough to be a character, like Katharine Hepburn, who at eighty-five speaks her mind and shuffles around in baggy brown pants. I can remember my grandmother's shaking her head and saying, "That Flo. She's a real character." I've already started wearing these sturdy oxford-type shoes, the kind you see in the L. L. Bean catalog. Maybe that's the first step. Next will come a voluminous black coat and excessively long earrings, and I'll carry a magnifying glass everywhere and peer at mosses and tree bark. I'll have a raspy laugh and will address my juniors as "Young man."

There's one problem, however, and it's something that Hepburn never had to deal with: About the time I stop being merely comfortable and start turning into an authentic character, Amanda's going to be hitting adolescence. You know what that means. We'll be getting ready for parents' night at the high school. It'll be a damp November evening, so I'll be tying a plastic rain bonnet around my head to match my galoshes and black coat. And she'll come in and shriek, "MO-therr, you are *not* going to wear that!"

Yes, dear, I am. And I'll probably have a better time than you will. It's *fun* to be old. You'll find out.

MOTHERING, MOMENT
BY MOMENT

A funny thing happened on the way to getting Amanda out of her bath last night. She was, as usual, sitting in the tub surrounded by about twenty unclothed Barbies and one very uncomfortable-looking Ken. "Hurry and wash up, or you'll look like one big wrinkled prune," I said.

"Want to hear the songs I made up?" she asked. Amanda has a masterly way of deflecting a direct order.

"Okay," I said.

She sang me several nonsensical compositions. I paid strict attention. As I did so, I thought, *This is what makes up "parenting," these little, seemingly insignificant moments. Your kid wants you to hear her song, and, because it's important to her, you decide to listen instead of saying, "Not now, I have to scrub the frying pan." And the moments heap up, one by one, and turn into years of raising a child. And you hope the good minutes, like this, outweigh the bad.*

When I read about "parenting" or "childrearing," I tend to think of the big, ongoing challenges: making sure that Amanda's diet somehow balances itself out into the four food groups, at least over the course of a week. Telling her about God. Warning her against strangers. Things like that. But much of what I do as a mother has to do with those small, sometimes split-second judgment calls. What I say. What I don't say. What I do right. What I do wrong and hope that God will smooth over.

This is what parenting is. . . .

Deciding to let Amanda miss a morning of school because she's been tired and needs to sleep in more than she needs to practice writing *s* in cursive.

Reflexively reminding her, "Only two," when she reaches for the box of cookies. I figure if I say it enough, something is going to get through.

Telling her, when she admits that she's afraid of the dark and is embarrassed by that fear, that I've read that the top five fears of children are: the dark, bugs, snakes, thunderstorms, and being left behind by their parents. Further telling her that I still don't like bugs. Laughing about bugs.

Jamming her hood on her head when the wind chill is below zero. Telling her, "Look, Mommy's wearing a hat, even though it scrunches my hair down flat. Sometimes it's more important to stay warm than look good, even for moms."

Leaving her alone when I sense she needs privacy.

Not leaving her alone when I sense she needs people.

Dropping everything to sit on the floor and look at her school papers, which the teacher wisely sends home only once a week.

Saying, "I'm sorry I yelled at you. I was wrong."

Handing her a toothbrush and barking "Brush!" when it would be easier to skip it before bed.

Heavyhandedly insisting that she'll LOVE some of the same books I read when I was a kid. Rejoicing (inwardly) when I'm proven right. Reading the rejects myself when I'm proven wrong.

Giving up on my efforts to convince her that she does not need thirty dolls on her bed. Earnestly trying to see the dolls as family, not clutter.

Agreeing to help out at the school library from time to time, even though I am congenitally unable to master the new checkout system of scanning a bar code. Just can't get that cute little wand to make the computer beep.

Refraining from waving excitedly at her when I work at school.

Looking at the picture she drew. Looking at the picture she drew. Looking . . .

Driving through a sleet storm when it would be easier to stay in, to make sure that she gets to her Wednesday night Pioneer program.

Asking her opinion.

Seizing opportunities to instruct her in "Dad and Mom's *Nonnegotiables*: We don't hit, we aren't mean, we never lie or cheat, we don't say bad words, and we think about other people's feelings. Thanking God when I see signs that the drumbeat of reminders is paying off.

Praying to God for help in my weakness when I realize that I am, whether I like it or not, a *role model*.

Giving her things to look forward to, like special trips.

Forcing myself on her with a washcloth when her mouth needs wiping. Letting her wipe it herself.

Not forcing her to sing in the children's choir, as much as her fond parents would love to see her perform up there in church.

Realizing she's different from me. Realizing that we're a lot alike. Loving her—and making sure she knows that—every day. And remembering that those moments, those days, add up to years, and years add up to a lifetime.

FLASH CARDS, FRANKLIN PIERCE, AND OTHER ADVENTURES IN LEARNING

D oes anyone else besides me think that the schools are demanding a great deal from parents these days?

When I was a kid back in the days when everything was in black and white, my parents hardly ever helped with homework, or went to school. My mother was a room parent for each of us kids, so occasionally she'd come with cupcakes for some party, or go along on a field trip. My dad looked at our report cards and gave us Ben Franklin fifty-cent pieces for our efforts. Once or twice a year he'd put on a dark suit and go to parents' night. This was an event on the order of the president's visiting some inner-city school for a photo op. I'm not sure that Dad even knew our teachers' names.

Mostly, though, we were pretty much on our own. Sink or swim. If it was a Sunday night and I was watching *Bonanza*, for instance, my mother might call out, "Got homework?" "Well, yeah," I'd mumble, and I'd go to my room and do homework. If I had to do a report on the Amazon Indians, Mom might say, "Go look it up in the encyclopedia." That was her input. The encyclopedia wasn't even very current. It featured black-and-white photo layouts on such subjects as "The Wonders of Steam" and "The League of Nations, the World's Hope."

Things are different now. A couple of weeks ago Amanda brought home her customary ream of school papers, newsletters, reminders, pleas for volunteer help. Tucked in the pile was a series of subtraction problems, with the suggestion that parents might want to make flash cards out of the problems so as to help their children keep up with math. Right now the second grade is learning about "regrouping," tens and ones columns so the children can understand the *principles* of subtraction and not just learn by rote.

"Do you want to do flash cards?" I asked my daughter. My apathetic tone strongly suggested that no, she did not want to do flash cards.

"No," she responded appropriately and went back to perusing her catalog of American Girls products. (Seventy-five dollars for one of those dolls. What are they made out of, bone china?)

I remember tens and ones from my childhood. I didn't understand the principles then and still don't. "Carry the one" was good enough for me. In my day we recited multiplication tables and learned that if Johnny has ten apples and Susie eight, Johnny's going to get a whopper of a bellyache.

I didn't throw away the subtraction paper. It's in one of my baskets, somewhere under the "Heart-Healthy Recipes" leaflet I picked up at the supermarket months ago. (I seem to have an entire corner of my house reserved for good intentions.) But I honestly do not know where I'm supposed to find the time to cut out flash cards and sit my daughter down and work on regrouping. Regrouping is something I do when I sit down after a long day and stare into space.

Reading is more problematic. When Amanda was an infant, I read an article in some magazine saying that it's never too early to start reading aloud to your kid. Hardly a week goes by that the school doesn't send home some directive reminding parents to read aloud to their child every day. I've always enjoyed reading, of course. I want my daughter to love books. But it was one thing to read *Pat the Bunny* aloud—or even *Curious George*. Now Amanda's into what she calls "chapter books," real books that have chapters and whole pages without illustrations.

So every night we curl up in her bed—and read 75- or even 150-page books. *I* read 150-page books, I should say. She listens. I drone on . . . and on . . . about mischievous Ramona Quimby or Samantha Parkington, a "bright Victorian beauty" from the American Girls series (the same outfit trying and succeeding in getting parents to buy their girls insanely expensive dolls), or *Harriet Tubman, Conductor on the Underground Railroad* or, Amanda's latest interest, Helen Keller. Amanda soaks up all this knowledge while my throat turns raspy and my back starts to ache and the circulation gets cut off from my legs. She asks questions like "What did Helen Keller sound like when she talked?" and "Sing slave songs for me."

Recently her class did reports on the presidents of the United States. They drew lots to select their guy, and Amanda wound up with Franklin Pierce. "What do you know about Franklin Pierce?" she asked when she came home one afternoon. I did not want to say that all I knew was that Hawkeye in *M*A*S*H* was named after him. "Well, he was president sometime before Lincoln, and he's not very famous," I managed. Amanda's report was, let us say, concise. However, she was not finished with me yet. Now she's always asking me to recite the presidents in order. I don't *know* the presidents in order. I know stuff like: Grover Cleveland was accused of fathering an illegitimate child, and Andrew Jackson's parrot said swear words. That is not the kind of parental support the school has in mind.

I suppose I could say, No, I can't read to you tonight. No, I can't help you draw a picture of Uranus with its rings. (In my day

Uranus didn't even have rings. When were they added?) But then I would be forfeiting my God-given role as My Child's First and Best Teacher. I would be contributing to our nation's educational slide vis-à-vis the Japanese, the Germans, the Luxembourgers and just about every other developed nation in the world.

And I haven't even mentioned the time that several other mothers and I were asked to go to school and help the teachers do something involving carving pumpkins and, so help me, *counting* pumpkin seeds to illustrate estimating and graphing. At the end of the hour my group was laboriously going, "Four hundred and ten, four hundred and eleven . . ." and everyone else was cleaning up, so I quickly suggested, "What say we call it an even five hundred and call it quits, guys?"

I know some of this comes with the territory. Just as my mother before me, I bake cupcakes and go along on field trips and faithfully attend school programs. I've liked all my daughter's teachers; I know they put in long hours, spend a lot of their own money for extras, and work under budgetary constraints unknown in the olden days when I was a schoolgirl. Schools need our help, and here I am whining.

But still . . . flash cards?

You know and I know that there WILL be mothers who will take the time to cut out and write flash cards with little Ryan or Kaitlyn. Who understand the essential meaning of subtraction, contrasted with people like me who often cut corners and just memorize. These models of scholastic support raise the stakes for the rest of us, who are then expected to follow suit. What's next, teaching our kids quantum theory at home in our spare time?

Oh, well. At least I make learning fun for Amanda. You should hear me ham it up on "Swing Low, Sweet Chariot." And I'm learning, too. Anything you'd like to know about Franklin Pierce?

FEAR NO EVIL

*Y*ou know her, or someone like her.

She is thirty-nine years old. She sings in the choir, alto section. Her husband has a beard and sings tenor. They have three young children. She tutors part-time, likes to read, is left-handed, drives a station wagon.

And she has cancer.

A couple of weeks ago we were talking after church. "If you think about it, you might pray for me," she said, almost offhandedly. "I'm having a biopsy tomorrow."

A few days later we are at a women's retreat. I'm pouring myself a glass of diet Dr. Pepper. In the corner a group of women are laughing at a video of *Sister Act*. I spot her and go up to her. "How'd it go?" I ask cheerfully, almost as if I were asking someone how they enjoyed their time at a health spa. I've known other women who had these biopsies. Almost always the answer is: "It was benign," or "I have fibroids." Something easily dealt with. Nothing to worry about. People our age don't get cancer. Cancer is something that your grandfather had, or a statistic you read about in the newspaper. Cancer doesn't happen to people like us, to women you know.

"The news is bad," she says quietly. "I have to have a

mastectomy next week." Only then do I notice the shadows around her eyes, as if she hadn't slept well.

Oh, God.

I struggle to say the right thing. What I want to ask is, "What is it like, knowing that you have this evil thing in your body?" Instead I ask about mechanics: When do you go in? What hospital? How long will the recovery period be? Small talk.

Then it is time for a get-acquainted icebreaker game, sharing our most embarrassing moment, favorite season, where we grew up. Things like that. We all howl with laughter as different women tell their stories. My friend—I'll call her Sue—laughs too, and even reveals an embarrassing moment of her own. I am glad she is here, surrounded by this love.

"I almost didn't come," she tells me as we resume our conversation later, "but my husband thought it would be good for me." God's timing, a thing of perfection.

"Well, they say laughter is healing," I say. I've heard that, but do I really believe it? Can laughter root out malignancy? Can friendship make people well? Malignancy. The word itself sounds almost demonic. Malign. Malevolent. Malnourished. Maladjusted. All those *mal* words that mean the opposite of what is supposed to be. *Mal* things want to hurt you.

She describes the situation to me. I sense a great weariness, as if she has already been over this ground a dozen times before. Inquiring minds want to know. Maybe I should let her have her privacy, but somehow I need to talk about it maybe even more than she does. Talking brings the bad thing, the malignancy, out into the light. Sitting around the card table, under the fluorescent lights of this basement rec room, we are like ancients around a campfire, and the darkness waits at the periphery.

And this is a black darkness indeed. The bad cells are too diffuse for a mere lumpectomy to work, I learn. There's a thirty-percent chance that the disease could spread to the other breast. They'll know more about follow-up treatment after the surgery. Her husband is trying to be strong for her, but he's scared. The children are a little too young to fully understand.

As she is talking, I imagine that I feel a twinge in my breast. But they say you don't feel anything in the early stages. It only starts hurting after it's too far gone for hope. Do I have risk factors? I have no familial history of the disease. I breast-fed Amanda. I don't eat a high-fat diet. But what about the peanut butter I sneak when I make Amanda's sandwiches? And I don't think I examine myself right . . . perhaps I'm secretly afraid of finding something. But they say you can't always feel the bad thing. The bad thing could be the size of a pea.

I look around at the women. Most of us are mothers and wives, approximately the same age. Most of us lead busy, sunlit lives. We are the generation that was better fed, better doctored, more privileged than any generation in history. Disease is an alien, almost anachronistic concept. If you get sick, it must be something you did wrong. Are they now thinking what I'm thinking? *If it could happen to Sue* . . .

I push the thought away. Get out of here. She'll be okay. It'll all turn out all right in the end. Lots of people survive this. I've even heard of entire clothes stores for women who've had mastectomies. They even sell swimsuits! Why, you just get on with your life. Don't you?

The weekend passes. As the retreat draws to a close, one of the women suggests that we all gather to pray for Sue. "I'm really glad," someone says to me. "I wouldn't have felt right if we hadn't." So others, too, feel this same need to *do* something tangible, to kiss the owie and make it all better.

But this isn't a skinned knee on one of our children. This is the big one. This is beyond our motherly competence. This is God's domain.

Someone, laughing, offers Sue a chair. She sits with an embarrassed smile. We all surround her and lay hands on her, this dear and gentle sister who is so much one of us, who is so grievously hurt. With voices choked with tears we pray for healing, for the doctors, for the family. Especially we pray for healing. Afterward I think of all the times we give ourselves an out, saying, "If it be Your will, Lord . . ." Not this time. This time we're praying that each and every one of the invading cells be routed, put to flight forever. Make her well, God.

Now *this* is a sister act. This is the sisters acting to help one of their own, and in the soft voices and gentle hands I sense something awesome and thunderous. Here, in this living room, we are doing nothing less than calling on the power of the Most High.

I think now of Sue preparing for her surgery this week. I pray again. Except for the time my father was sick, I've never prayed so hard or so often for anything, and I know others are praying similarly. I still feel as if an evil intruder has broken into our sunlit world. But now I feel as if he might be vanquished— that there is hope. God is here and He is good. And we, we of the soft voices and small hands and easy tears, are helping Him do His work. And I am not as afraid—not for Sue, not for any of us.

THE MAN WHO SPILLED
HIS SPAGHETTI, AND
OTHER CONVICTING
MOMENTS

*H*as this ever happened to you?

You think you're in pretty good control of your life. You think you've enjoyed a few successes. You're content that you're where God wants you to be. Your children are well and happy. You're keeping ahead of the dust balls. You've been asked to head an interesting committee at church.

Then you meet someone who's much more accomplished and in control than YOU will ever be, and something inside sort of fizzles.

Let's say it's a nice, warm day. You've taken your children to the park for a picnic. They're playing on the climbing equipment, and you strike up a conversation with one of the other mothers. This other mother is wearing short shorts and looks like an advertisement for *Women's Workout World*. You shift around on the bench so your cellulite smooths out and think, *Well, she's probably all sinew and no brain*. Then she tells you she's working on her degree in molecular biology at a downtown university and today's her day off. You, of course, can hardly find time to finish the *Reader's Digest* in the bathroom, and you haven't been to the city in months, though you keep telling yourself you should. As it is, though, the last stimulating family outing you had was a trip to the mall to see the Audio-Animatronic plastic dinosaurs.

Or one of your best friends, the one you always counted on to be as slothful as yourself, lets you down. She takes up stenciling and re-does all her children's bedrooms in cute little patterns. As she proudly shows you the results of her hard work, you think of the dead-insect splotches on your daughter's ceiling. You've been meaning to get to those for a couple of years now, but it involves hauling a ladder into the house because the ceiling is high and, well, no one looks at your *ceilings*, do they?

Or a couple you know at church tells you and your husband how they took the complete Larry Burkett course in personal finance and now have eliminated all their debt except their mortgage, save prodigious amounts every month, and still manage to support three missionary families, all without the wife having to go back to work. Oh, and their daughter is getting a full ride to Wheaton, so they won't have to borrow for college. You give them a forced smile and congratulate them on being such prudent stewards. Meanwhile, you're recalling the time that you and your husband had to go throughout the house, picking pennies off the floor, digging in drawers, scrounging in coat pockets—just to amass enough cash to buy milk.

Or, as happened to me a while ago, you're sitting at a long table in your daughter's school gym, enjoying a PTA spaghetti fund-raiser. A woman sits down near you, and she is perfect. Porcelain-doll face, white skin, adorable little nose. Flawless make-up, just the right amount of eyeshadow and blush. (Some of us can never seem to get that right. It's always too much or not enough.) Beautiful patterned sweater, probably eighty bucks in the Eddie Bauer catalog. Nails done. Huge wedding ring. She looks affluent, tasteful, put together. She smiles and talks animatedly with the people around her. She reminds you of every popular girl you ever envied in high school.

This is a woman who never wears pantyhose with holes in the feet, whose children never talk back, who never misses her quiet time. Watch her eat spaghetti, how she rolls it so perfectly and eats it so daintily. You wonder if you have red sauce around your mouth, and you scrape at your face, just in case. You don't know anyone you're sitting with, so just to look social and not stare emptily into space, you engage your daughter in prolonged conversation. (She, of course, is getting restless and wants to go check out the dessert table.)

The in-control person. The more-successful-than-you person. The person who has accomplished what you have not; the woman who magically extracts three extra hours from her day. They're everywhere, like flies in August, like pizza places in strip malls. They make a mockery of your feeble triumphs. They make you feel insecure and slightly disheveled.

I think about this now, and then I remember that there was a man sitting at our table at the spaghetti supper.

He was probably in his sixties but looked much older. Lank, white hair hung down into his gaunt face. His hands shook as he tried to get the spaghetti to his mouth; in fact, his whole body trembled. He had some sort of palsy, or maybe Parkinson's disease. There was something distinguished-looking about him, a fineness of feature, as if he might have been a professor or scientist at one time. The people with him were helping him eat, bringing him coffee.

I did not want to stare, and squeezed Amanda's hand under the table to give her the same message. She's at an age where she's fascinated by infirmities.

This man was definitely not in control. Not flawless. Accomplished, maybe; but that was a long time ago.

I remember all this now as I look toward a hectic week of

how-am-I-going-to-get-it-all-done, I-hope-the-check-comes-today, why-am-I-not-like-those-other-women worry and insecurity. I realize again that God does not give a rip about stenciled bedrooms and master's degrees and manicures. I think about how much God loves that palsied man spilling his spaghetti all over; how, in God's eyes, that man is a remarkable creature, someone to be loved, cared for, honored. And I feel ashamed.

Why do I worry about those more "accomplished"? What *is* accomplishment, anyway? Why can I not see as God sees?

This is a tough one, because I *do* care about a nicely decorated home, groomed nails, personal and professional achievement. I set high standards for myself and work energetically to live up to them. Sometimes I even come close. Other times . . . Well, the insect splotches are still there.

I guess I'm still trying to grow into God's lenses. They're a little big for me, and they'll never fit perfectly here on earth. But I hope that someday, by His mercy, I'll look at everyone as unique, gifted, special—and imperfect, not always in control. The woman in shorts, the busy-bee stenciler, the prudent stewards, the man eating spaghetti, even the woman in the Eddie Bauer sweater . . . We're all struggling in our own ways, but God loves us anyway. No strings attached. He loves *me*, even with my faulty vision.

And He doesn't want me to be like anyone else!

I know that in my head. Slowly, and at a late date, that idea may finally be finding its way into my heart, too.

OLD STEELHANDS
ATTACKS THE
PLAGUE GERMS

*H*usbands are great to have around. For love, for companionship, for laughter, for shared faith and shared parenting, and shared bed. And for dirty jobs.

I realized this not long ago when I was cleaning the bathroom. (If you are squeamish, skip to the next chapter.) I like a sparkling clean bathroom, maybe to compensate for the fact that I wish I had a huge old-fashioned lavatory with a pedestal sink, chicken-wire tile and matching dark-green accessories, but I don't. I scrub everything—the bathtub, the sink, the mirror, the floor, the toilet. I put out fresh color-coordinated towels and buy air fresheners disguised as blue geese. I even have this duster on a long pole that kills cobwebs. (When Amanda was a little girl, she thought cobwebs were alive. Once she asked, "Do cobwebs buzz?" So now I think of them as a primitive life form infesting my house. It's a great incentive to dust.)

There is, however, one bathroom chore I refuse to perform. You know how this gunk collects on the base of the toilet and on the floor around and behind it, especially if you have hard water? I'm not going to give you a graphic description. You know what I'm talking about. It's a really disgusting job to clean it up, plus we have a little crack in the base of the toilet where *something* gets trapped. I could just leave it, but then I know some perfect-homemaker friend would ask to use the facilities and come running out going *AAGGGHHH! Brown gunk!* just when I was serving the ladies my best chicken-and-grape salad. Not only that, no less an authority than Dave Barry once said that plague germs fester down there. Ever since then I've worried about mutant antigens spawning in the dark recesses of my bathroom, and my daughter tends to have allergies anyway, so you're talking about lives at stake here.

This is where a husband comes in. After I've finished the bathroom to my satisfaction, I call for him, very sweetly. "Babe," I say, "could you do me a really big favor?"

"Sure," he says, a little warily.

Even though I have approached him in this way many times before, I act as though I've given this a lot of thought and only with great reluctance, having exhausted all other alternatives, am I making this request. "Um, I can't reach around the back of the toilet. My arms are too short. Would you mind scrubbing for me down there? I'll get you a nice clean rag and some Lysol."

"Why do we have to clean in back? No one can see it."

Reasonable enough. But I cannot explain to him that there are certain areas of my life where, if they are under control, I feel somehow virtuous and competent. Being stocked up on certain things—postage stamps, pantyhose, bath soap—gives me a soothing sense of security and order. Knowing that I have cared enough to clean where no one will ever see, makes me feel like I've gone the extra mile, that I am not just a person who does things for show. I may stuff things under the bed, but by gum, you could *eat* off the tile in my john; therefore, I am a good person.

My husband feels the same way about having enough gas in the car and snack food in the pantry, but he cannot relate to my bathroom fetish. So I hand him the big old towel that I reserve for serious scrubbing and say, "It's important to me, that's all. And you're better at it than I am."

The trump card!

He capitulates and scrubs. "Oh, and while you're at it," I say over my shoulder as I depart feeling strangely warmed, "you might want to wipe the baseboard back there. And really get in those tile cracks."

Funny thing is, I'm not really being manipulative when I say he's better at such tasks. He's persistent, for one thing. He has this Dutch doggedness that keeps at a task until it's done right. Whereas I, with my more mercurial Irish temperament, get bored and give up if I can't get something spotless with a few squirts of the spray bottle, like in the commercials. We make a great team.

Also, my husband has been known to bench-press more than two hundred pounds. He's really strong, especially in the hands. You wouldn't necessarily know it because he's more wiry than burly, and this can give people nasty surprises. Sometimes when we greet in church and he shakes hands, older ladies move away from us smiling fixedly and surreptitiously massaging their mashed fingers. I've had to show him how to shake hands as I've heard Queen Elizabeth does, with about three fingers limply extended. Nothing like maiming the body of Christ with the right hand of fellowship. But this facility can be put to good use around the house, especially for chores I have no interest in.

Just this morning, in fact, I was cleaning up around the kitchen when I noticed the sink was covered with an odd sort of wax, a carapace, if you will. I have no idea where it came from, but I'm suspicious of the cucumbers I peeled a few nights ago. The amount of wax they spray on those cukes nowadays would keep all the chiffoniers in Mount Vernon gleaming for a year. Anyhow, I sprayed it, and nothing happened. I scraped at it once or twice with my fingernails, and nothing happened. Time to call in Old Steelhands.

"Lover, are you busy?" I trilled out.

"Well, I just shoveled the driveway and thought I might get a nice cup of—"

I looked out the window. "Oooh, good job." Shameless creature! "I was wondering if you had any idea where this wax came from."

What male can resist an appeal to his superior knowledge, especially in these egalitarian times? Not my male. He frowned at the sink and considered. "Boy, it's hard to say. You want me to scrub it off, don't you?"

I think he's catching on, folks. He knows me too well. Time to drop the helpless act. "Yes. I don't want to do it. Here's the scrubber."

And again I say, husbands are great to have around. For affection, for financial support, for protection, for chores, for honesty.

And, thanks to him, I'm starting to feel more caught up around the house. It's a good thing, too, because pretty soon he'll have his work cut out for him again. It's almost spring—bug season. Just think, if those hands of steel can send little old ladies reeling away into the sanctuary on Sunday morning, imagine what they could do to one of those thousand-leggers unfortunate enough to blunder into our bathtub. Vive la différence!

AT HOME AND
OUT OF IT?

*I*t's funny how we second-guess even our good decisions
sometimes.

I went into my former office the other day to take care of
some business. I dressed up, took my briefcase, got out early. I
was surprised at how good it felt, having to be somewhere at an
appointed time. Computer keys clicked with precision, secretaries
answered telephones, the copier hummed, and well-dressed
people strode purposefully about. I looked in at my old office, the
corner office I had worked hard to attain, now occupied by
someone else. I noticed that the plant in the window was
flourishing, in contrast to when I was tending it and it barely hung
in . . . never dying—but hardly thriving, either. The plant hadn't
missed me.

But had I missed my office?

I have a friend who's a vice-president at a consulting firm.
She flies around giving seminars on managing change. She isn't
available much during the week to get together; she's out of town
or at her office, supervising things. She's organized, competent,
articulate. I can imagine her standing at a lectern in some hotel
meeting room talking to a group of men in suits. I used to be more

like that, but I have a different kind of life now. Sometimes I look at her or the other working women in my church and wonder if I've lost my edge by working at home these last couple of years. Am I still organized and competent?

Just after lunch today (macaroni and cheese in the kitchen with Amanda) I was downtown doing errands in our community. I had on the at-home mom's version of formal wear: denim skirt, flats, cardigan sweater. I watched the office workers going back to their jobs in suits and smart dresses and jewelry. *They* had probably gone to a restaurant for their lunch, and it wasn't macaroni and cheese with a kid making second-grade jokes. Maybe a seafood salad paid for with the corporate credit card. I looked at them and felt . . . unstructured. Housewifely. Out of the loop.

Me?

Now when I get up in the morning, my main concern is prying Amanda out of bed. When the phone rings, it is as likely to be someone wanting me to do something for school or church as it is a work-related call. When there's a school holiday—as seems to occur with marked frequency nowadays—I forget that most of the adult world, except maybe local government bureaucrats, does not take off to celebrate Casimir Pulaski's contributions to American history—that people are actually in their offices, earning a salary.

How my life has changed! I used to earn a regular paycheck, and I did not have to spend any of it on manila envelopes and pens and scratch paper. I could scrawl "FILE" on a folder and behold, it was done—by someone else. Now I have a home office with piles. My filing system. Now I spend my own money at the stationery store. Sometimes I remember to save the receipt for tax purposes, sometimes I forget. I save old manila envelopes and recycle them. My answering machine screens my calls (which are sometimes interrupted by a small person picking up the extension and breathing through her mouth into the receiver). When I talk to a friend from my old office, I have to remind myself that she is at work and does not have unlimited time to spend on chitchat.

I work, too, of course, and work hard, but my time is more my own. I nap when I'm tired. I volunteer for church stuff now. I'm at school more. We entertain more. Amanda's friends tend to congregate here. Some days, especially during the summer, I feel like the neighborhood mom whose presence—and popsicles—draw children as sugar water draws butterflies.

It sounds like a nice life, all this flexibility, and it is. It sounds like the kind of life I used to envy when I was stuck in an office on a warm spring day. But still, some mornings when I go out to get the paper in my robe and see the neighbors backing out of their driveways to go to work, I wonder if the time will come when I want to jump back into that rushing stream, get out of the house and away from the dirty dishes, go to meetings, and make important decisions. I could maybe make more money; then we could afford to get Chinese takeout once in a while instead of saving coupons and cooking from scratch (like spaghetti soup).

I have begun to see why at-home moms can get defensive; why they feel at best, ignored—and at worst, looked down upon by the world. The world talks about corporate day-care centers and dual-income households and how no one makes dinner anymore. The world doesn't even recognize staying home as an option. Of course you work. Doesn't everybody, these days? This isn't the '50s. Ozzie and Harriet, what jerks. Kids get by. They adjust.

You listen to that stuff enough, especially if you once were part of that corporate world, and you begin to doubt your choice. On the days I feel poor and forgotten, I want to hear my daughter say, "Thank you for quitting your job, Mommy. Thank you for sacrificing to be with me."

Naturally I don't hear that, and that's maybe as it should

be. She accepts that I'm there for her, that we can walk to and from school together in good weather, that I don't have to make special arrangements when she's home, sick. I've been *that* route, having to call a male supervisor and say: Sorry, my child is ill, and no, no one else can take care of her, and I apologize for her needing me, but I'll work extra hard to make up for my absence.

Hmmm.

When I start remembering those days, times when I almost had to justify my role as a mother, I begin to feel grateful. Grateful that I am able to pursue my craft from home, grateful that we don't have a lot of expensive "wants," grateful for the support of friends who have made similar decisions, grateful for a church that doesn't judge either mothers at home or working moms but brings us together as sisters in the Lord.

I was able to finish up my office business in a couple of hours. I said good-bye to my former co-workers, went home, and changed clothes. I didn't belong there anymore. I belong here— piled-up dishes, disorganized home office, endless pb&j's and all.

And my life hasn't *entirely* changed: My plants here at home don't like me, either.

MY HOUSE HAS IT IN FOR ME

When my husband and I presented our certified check and signed twenty-seven different documents at the closing on our house and in turn received house keys, deed, and sundry other papers, we proudly joined the ranks of the propertied classes. No more renting. No more living under the guy who cranked up the bass speaker on his stereo at three in the morning. No more worrying about our toddler's defacing the landlord's white walls.

We were proud of our little home. Still are. I love this house, the corner lot, the flowers, the interesting moldings and arches, my blue kitchen. God has provided, and we are grateful. However, more than six years of home ownership has taught me that houses have it in for you.

Houses eat money. When you own your own home, the phrase "disposable income" becomes a hollow mockery. Last week our friend Tom the Handyman was down in our basement doing something with noisy machinery as he dismantled our very old, very clogged pipes (hair from Amanda's Little Mermaid doll was the culprit) and replaced them with shiny new plastic piping. *Urp!* Another several hundred dollars swallowed. The other day Amanda showed me a hole in the sole of her Minnie Mouse canvas shoes. My child will have to wear flapping cardboard soles because we are spending money on this inanimate assemblage of brick and plaster and new kitchen tile that is already starting to heave up in places.

Every time you get a few dollars ahead—a tax refund, a birthday gift of cash, whatever—the house knows. It goes, "Heh heh. You think you have money. But what you don't know is that the heat exchanger in the furnace has cracked and you and your loved ones are living on borrowed time. Soon, unless you SPEND MONEY, your living space will be flooded with deadly fumes. Feeling a bit sleepy, are we?"

Just an aside: Cars are the same way. It's almost worse, because at least houses appreciate in value, thereby giving you something back for all your loving care and hemorrhage of money. But cars, now. They hate you. It's as if they're hissing, "Every day I am becoming less and less valuable. Soon I will bring you no monetary recompense whatsoever. But, just out of sheer spite, I wish to make you poor. Hear that pinging?"

On the other hand, you can get rid of a car. It's harder to get rid of a house. You're sort of stuck with it, and the house knows that full well. So in addition to enormous structural expenditures, the house also mocks you with continuous clutter and never-ending chores.

Last year I had noble intentions. I was going to embark on an enormous cleaning binge—drapes to the dry cleaner, junk out of the basement, files created for financial, household, church, professional records.

The house knew.

The house knew and mustered its forces. The first place I set out to clean was Amanda's closet. I looked at the vaporizer sitting on the top shelf. It needs to be cleaned out, because, I have heard, a vaporizer is the perfect culture medium for the pneumococcus bacillus. I looked at the jumble of mismated shoes and

Barbie-doll heads and the remains of old, old Vacation Bible School projects like rotini necklaces, and I sighed, or maybe it was a death rattle, signaling the demise of my hopes for a clean and organized abode. Then, as I was closing the door, I caught my finger between the two panels that fold in.

So now it has come to this. My house is out to injure me. After all I've done for it—saved it from the green and orange wallpaper that was here when we moved in, filled it with the happy shouts of children at play. Our pastor even blessed it when we first moved in and gave a housewarming.

After this "accident," I decided that the best recourse was to not care, not to try so hard. Give up on the basement. Liberate myself from worrying about the weeds behind the garage. My mother always advised me to ignore the mean kids who teased. Maybe I should ignore my mean house.

I've been working on this attitude, and mostly I've felt better. Then I went to take a shower this morning—and the round thing to turn on the water came off in my hand.

You can't win. On the other hand, it could be worse. I could still be listening to rock-and-roll at three in the morning.

THE CAR CRASH THAT TURNED INTO A PARTY

I never thought a car accident could be so much fun.

It must have been about five or so on a late-summer afternoon. I was in the kitchen putting potatoes on to boil for supper. Amanda was across the street, playing. The windows were open, letting in balmy breezes. Suddenly I heard a *screeeech* of tires, followed by the crash of metal on metal and the sound of glass shattering. I darted to the phone and dialed 911, feeling important and grave. "There's been an accident around President and Harrison," I said breathlessly. Any injuries? "I don't know, but it sounded bad."

There's an instinct every mother has when something like this happens—the instinct to make sure that her own child is safe, that the wail of the siren isn't a summons with her name on it. I ran out the back door and looked around. There she was, running up to the corner with her friends. There, too, passed an excited stream of humanity—mothers pushing strollers, dads carrying kids on their shoulders, neighbors I hadn't seen in months. You would have thought the Fourth of July parade was going to march down the street any minute.

"Mom!" Amanda yelled when she spotted me. "Did you hear the crash? Wasn't it awesome? Megan's mom called 911!"

"So did I."

"Really? What was it like? What did they say? Weren't you scared?" *Just for a split-second*, I thought and grabbed her hand. "Stay with me."

A car had hit a light pole, which now lay halfway across the roadway. I was amazed to see Bob, our quiet next-door neighbor who always keeps to himself, directing traffic around the mess with the aplomb of a Manhattan cop. The things you find out about people at a time of crisis.

The crowd of onlookers swelled. It was as if every house in the vicinity was disgorging its contents. Fritz appeared and started talking to Randy, who lives a block away and works in Christian publishing. Usually we never see him around, but there he was with his small boys. No one was hurt, Randy said. Apparently the car had been trying to make a left turn. He pointed to a couple of very shaken-looking teenage girls across the street.

By now the police had arrived. When it became obvious that the accident wasn't truly serious—only interesting—the mood of the crowd turned festive. One guy was describing the scene to someone on his cordless phone. I waved gaily as a couple of people I knew drove slowly by, rubbernecking. Several boys of about ten described with relish exactly what happened: "The car went out of control *right there*. See the skid marks? And then this other car had to slam on its brakes, and then . . ."

Here came Donna from the next street over, trailed as usual by her coterie of several small children. Donna always looks as though she's having her own parade. "Boy, I hate to think of what's going to happen to that girl when her dad finds out," she said, shaking her head. "I know what *my* dad would have done."

The ten-year-old boys, showing off, started running into the street. I restrained Amanda, who loves nothing more than to be at the center of things, from following suit. "Please, everybody, stay back," said a policeman who looked to be about twenty. (Why do all policemen look young enough to be your nephew? What ever happened to all the old, avuncular Officer O'Malley types? Why do they all wear mustaches?)

There was almost a carnival atmosphere. I half expected to see balloon vendors and hawkers yelling: "Red hots! Get yer red hots!" People who usually barely acknowledge one another's existence were chatting away like friends at a college reunion. One of the other moms looked around and said, "We must really be hard up for entertainment."

I watched the people watching the street maintenance crew sweep up the debris. The teenage driver's father had now arrived and was consoling his daughter. I could read his face and gestures clearly: Don't worry about the car, the insurance will take care of it. At least you're okay! Come on, let's go home. I thought about Amanda, eight years away from getting her license. My little daredevil, who likes to hang from the highest monkey bars at school. And I knew exactly how that father felt.

The crowd was beginning to drift away. I stayed a little longer, chatting with some of the other women. It felt . . . nice, traditional. Back-fence stuff. I remembered my own growing-up, how all the neighborhood kids were always out playing in summer, how my mother was friends with most of the other moms. I remembered the time that Fritz and I were at the video store when a nice-looking young couple greeted us cordially. "Who were they?" I asked him when we got in the car. "They live in that white house across the street," he said.

What's changed? Why does it take a car crash to bring people together? Why do I not know most of my neighbors that well, even though we've lived here five years and I'm home much of the time and a lot of the other women are, too? Where *is* everybody? And why does the center of people's lives always have to be somewhere other than the home, the yard, the block? Why are we all so busy?

Now the lightpole lay on the grass, guarded by a barricade. You'd hardly know anything had happened here. I remembered my potatoes and hoped that Fritz had turned them down. Reluctantly I called for Amanda. Even *she* had lost interest in the accident and had run off. Only a few other mothers and I were left. We all made noises about how we'd "better get supper on the table" and, "Isn't it starting to get dark early?" and "We'll see you around the neighborhood."

I hope so. I really do.

AMANDA LEARNS
ABOUT IT

Well, it finally happened.

I had walked Amanda and Lindsay the Neighbor Child home from school. On the way, they had stopped off to see one of their favorite neighborhood dogs and the dog's person, a widow who lives alone in an interesting, large house. "You can go, Mom," Amanda said with a gesture of dismissal.

So I went.

Later that afternoon, after Neighbor Child had gone home, I asked Amanda if she had had fun at Mrs. Ross's. "Oh, she wasn't there," she said.

"So what did you do?"

"We sat on her step and talked. Lindsay told me about a book she had read, about something a man does to a woman."

Here it came.

Amanda, giggling, proceeded to describe, rather loosely, what a man does to a woman. "Isn't that funny?" Then she changed the subject. Clearly she was not especially curious.

As I stood there in the dining room holding her "wraps" (as teachers always call them), my life as a mother flashed before my eyes. For such a time as this have I been preparing for eight years. Is now the existential moment of truth? Do I sit down with her, put my arm around her, and say, "Well, sweet girl, let me tell you how it is"? Lindsay is two years older, a seasoned ten (and what has *she* been reading, anyway?). I remembered my husband's telling me that his parents never did teach him about It. "I learned about it from boys at camp," he said. "I thought it sounded gross." I recalled my own mother, when I was in about fifth grade, imparting information in the most, um, barebones way, and my subsequent wildly inaccurate mental pictures.

Had I been shirking my responsibility? Now my child was, almost literally, picking up information on the street, from a girl who hardly qualifies as the local Dr. Joyce Brothers.

I decided to do what has usually worked in the past: go with my instinct. All right, all right, cop out. But what my instinct told me was that she wasn't really interested or disturbed or puzzled. You know these things about your kid. She had been briefly amused, and now she was on to other things, so I let it go.

This time.

But I knew the moment would come. Otherwise, I just knew, some fifth-grader of uncertain parentage, wearing an earring and Guns 'N Roses T-shirt, would sidle up to my girl on the school playground and hiss, "Hey, kid. Guess what? Your mom and dad *did it!*" And Amanda would have one of two reactions: either she'd thrash the guy to defend the family honor—or she'd widen her green eyes and say, "Really? What's *that?*"

Except my child is only in second grade. Too young. It's too early.

I mentally reviewed what she did know and when she knew it. She knows the right names for parts of the anatomy. I read in an article by a Christian sex therapist that it was important to dispassionately teach children the clinical names, so that God's gift of the physical body isn't cloaked in smirking euphemism. So once when Amanda was taking a bath and referred inaccurately to one of her parts, I mumbled, "No, that's your . . . that's your . . ." and then I blurted out the correct term and quickly covered myself by dropping the shampoo bottle on my foot.

She knows that grown-ups sometimes kiss when they really like each other, like when Beauty kissed the Beast and he turned into a prince. She's seen college students walk hand in hand by our house. *"They're* boyfriend and girlfriend," she'll report to me with satisfaction.

I have also told her about falling in love, that when you fall in love you want to live together always, like her mommy and daddy did, and you get married and have children, and that hugging and kissing are best after you're husband and wife. This, I have told her, is God's way. She knows that God thought of her and gave her to us, that He knew her even before she was born.

However, I'm not sure she quite sees her aging parents as romantic icons. Her daddy is someone who hauls out the garbage, cuts himself shaving, buys her junk food at the supermarket. Her mom reads Ramona books to her and tells her she has to wear skirts to Sunday school and yells at her daddy for buying junk food at the supermarket. Sure, Mom and Dad hug each other, but I suspect that to Amanda, our hugs communicate as much sex as, say, Leonid Brezhnev embracing Alexei Kosygin. Not the same as the pretty young college girl and her smitten swain out for a springtime stroll.

TV? Not in our house. Somewhat to my surprise, I have become decidedly illiberal on that score. Amanda used to watch reruns of "family-oriented" sitcoms. Then one day I realized that some of these programs contained more sexual innuendo than the mind of a fourteen-year-old boy. Since then we've limited her viewing to the likes of *Anne of Green Gables* and *The Chronicles of Narnia*: Thank God for the invention of the VCR!

What does Amanda know? Not much. Not yet. Oh, there's a boy at school she sort of likes and who likes her back.

They hurl snowballs at each other and call each other names. Once when she dropped her colored pencils on the classroom floor, her youthful protector said, "*I'll* pick them up for her!" He's a nice boy from a Christian home. I sometimes envision an Anne Shirley-Gilbert Blythe school days romance blossoming between the two someday and wonder if his parents would go along with an arranged marriage. But I don't push it. These things have a way of backfiring, and I wouldn't want to drive her to the leering fifth-grader with the earring.

Right now she's just a little kid, after all, despite her know-it-all bravado. I've heard all about how we're robbing our children of their childhood, and I refuse to be a party to the crime. Soon enough—next month, next year—the day will come when we'll be driving together or cleaning her room. (These things usually work better when you have something else to occupy your focus.) I'll clear my throat and say, "You know, honey, a wonderful thing happens when a husband loves a wife, and a wife loves a husband, and they decide that they love each other so much that they want to create a new life out of that love, and this is how it happens and if there's anything you want to know, just ask me."

And she'll look at me and say scornfully, "Oh, Mom, I've known that for *years*." And I'll be struggling to regain my pose of all-wise mother, and then she'll probably say, "But you and Daddy didn't do it that yucky way. God just put me in you. Right?"

Yes, dear. God certainly did.

BLESSED BE THE
LITTLE CHILDREN

*A*manda, get up!"
"Amanda, go to bed!"
"Amanda, eat your carrots!"

After she had wet her bed, four-year-old Samantha was beaten by her mother's live-in boyfriend. The child later died of massive internal injuries.

"Mommy, I have to get Valentines."
"Oh, brother. Remember how long it took you to make them last year?"

David and Sharon Schoo were indicted by a grand jury on thirty-nine counts of child neglect and endangering a child's life. The couple, who gained nationwide notoriety when they left their two daughters home alone for nine days while they vacationed in Mexico, have been accused of locking their older daughter in their crawl space. The children are in foster care.

"Amanda, hurry up. Why are you such a dawdler?"

"But Mommy, I—"
"Never mind! Come on!"

*A two-year-old New York boy was killed in an apartment fire.
It is believed that the fire started when he and his sister were playing
with a lighter. Mother Linda Gomez said that she was unable to find
care for the children while she was at work.*

I am taking Amanda back to school after lunch. I am glad
she can come home, have a break in her day, eat hot soup instead
of sitting in the noisy gym eating pb&j and not eating her apple.
Besides, she says, there's a first grader named Ben who burps in
her ear. I walk her into the school, pat her on the shoulder and
leave. Here comes the bus full of kindergarteners from the low-
income apartments. They scamper off in their bright jackets and
backpacks—black and Hispanic and Anglo children. So sweet and
fresh and hopeful. I smile at them; then suddenly I am weeping as
I get in the car. What will become of these kindergarteners? That
boy there, will he join a gang? That girl, will she get pregnant? Do
they return to empty apartments, or to live-in boyfriends with
short fuses?

And then I am angry. Angrier because I don't know whom
to be angry at. I go home and look at Amanda's tidy pink room
with the shelves full of books we've bought for her and have read
to her since she was an infant. The prism in her window is spraying
rainbows all over the walls. "Blessed be the little children, sweet
and fresh from Heaven above," reads a plaque someone made for
her when she was born.

I think of all the Samanthas, all the Schoos, all the
Gomezes, all the children that Amanda has already learned to refer
to as "bus kids." Us and them, neighborhood kids and bus kids. I
think of Julian, the apartment kid who hit Amanda on the
playground. There's a lot more of that at school this year, and I'm

told it's because there are too many bus kids going to a small neighborhood school that was never meant to accommodate them—and their problems. I wish they'd go away. I wish someone could help them. I don't know what I can do. And I don't want them to hit my daughter.

"This is reality today," someone said to me. I don't like reality. I want to pretend it's the 1950s.

Then I look in the mirror and see a great big plank sticking out of my eye. It doesn't become me. I turn away.

Back at school, picking Amanda up, I don't look at the kids being herded onto the buses. I walk straight to my child's classroom, where she is slowly getting ready, one of the last to leave. I ask to see the math projects she's been working on, the stories the teacher has been reading to them. I don't hurry her. We take advantage of this midwinter sunshine and walk home together, swinging hands as we walk. It's a safe neighborhood. When we get home, I close the door behind us and ask if she'd like to bake some cookies.

A SPLASH OF COLD WATER

S ometimes God has a way of shaking us awake.
I was loading the dishwasher. Amanda was in the living
room having an argument with two playmates. (Psychologists call it
"triangulation," but the rest of the world calls it three's a crowd,
especially when all three are under ten years old.) I was wondering
whether I should step in as mediator when the phone rang. I
answered distractedly, assuming it would be one of the children's
parents summoning them home, but it was Nancy.

"How are you?" she asked. "If I never called you, I would
never find out."

Nancy. Honest, heart-on-sleeve, one-of-a-kind Nancy
who hangs prisms in her windows and wears sweatshirts that say
"When I Am an Old Lady I Shall Wear Purple." When I decided to
quit my job, Nancy took me out for a celebration at White Castle.
When I was feeling snowed under with work, Nancy sent me a
hilarious card. When several of us were at Nancy's for talk and
munchies one night and I started missing my dad, who had died a
few months before, she held me while I wept. Nancy remembers
my birthday. Nancy tends our parakeets when we go on vacation.
Nancy calls me.

I told Nancy that I had been going crazy with book work
and church commitments and I had speaking engagements coming

up and, well, Nance, you know how it is. But I've been thinking of you. (I did not add, thinking of you—and feeling guilty.)

Nancy was sympathetic. We talked, she in her kitchen and I in mine, *her* parakeet squawking in the background and my crowd of three fighting in the background. As usual we dived right into things significant to each of us. I told her of my plan to write a book about the hidden loneliness of the Christian woman and the need to connect. Paused. Laughed ruefully about setting myself up as an expert on friendship. Ha-ha, who do I think I am? Nancy laughed, too.

As the conversation drew to a close, I again apologized for not keeping in closer touch. "Well, sometimes I do think, if she's not going to call me then why should I call her?" Nancy admitted. "But . . ."

But then Nancy takes the initiative, and I do not. Not often enough.

It's easy to say that Nancy, with no children at home now, has more time than I do. It's easy to say that I'm being too hard on myself, that just the other day a friend with four kids said, "I don't call *anybody* just to say 'How are you?'" Here is the truth: I hurt someone I care about, and I feel awful about it.

Later that evening we returned from shopping to find a message from Nancy on the answering machine. She wanted to tell me that she had a book on friendship by a Christian counselor and I was welcome to borrow it if I wanted.

Faithful Nancy. She did not have to do that.

God gave me a good talking-to through my friend . . . and, as usual, it came at a time when I was feeling pretty proud of myself for being so good at juggling so many things. He reminded me that I sometimes feel overly guilty about the wrong things (how my house looks) and not guilty enough about the right things. He showed me that while I can waste a lot of time feeling unloved and needy, there might be someone who needs *me*.

I thought again about Sue, my friend from church who had undergone a mastectomy. I thought of the way life's journey can take some hairpin turns. I remembered something I had read, that people should ask themselves how they would like to be eulogized at their memorial service. Would I want someone to stand up and say, "She always met her deadlines"? Or, "She was never too busy for laughs and sliders"?

Yes, I am busy. Realistically I just can't spend as much time with my friends as I would like. Nor they with me. But I can let them know, as Nancy did, that I am *there* for them. I can pray for them, drop them a note, leave a funny message on their machine. I can be faithful—as God is faithful.

That, you see, is the second part of the story. God loves me—loves us—so much that, as we parents do with our own children, He sometimes has to intervene to save us from ourselves, as much as we may resist. If it were up to Amanda, she would eat four cookies at one sitting. I sometimes have to forcibly pry the bag out of her grasp and say, "No more." She doesn't like it, but there's a part of her, that growing-up part, that concedes that sometimes, Mom does know best.

God always knows best. I would always prefer a pat on the back to a splash of cold water, a "Well done!" to a "Try again," but sometimes that cold water of truth can shake me out of complacency and help me grow into the woman God would have me become.

The wonderful thing is that this Father helps us with the growing. He doesn't just give us a talking-to and leave. He's right there with us, cheering us on.

So I think I'll drop by Nancy's next week and pick up that book. Who knows? Maybe she'll even have a bag of sliders in the freezer ready for unexpected company. They'd defrost a lot quicker than a casserole.

BUT CAN YOU PUT CATSUP ON IT?

D oes it sometimes seem to you as if those experts who lay down the guidelines for the "ideal American diet" have (a) unlimited time; (b) unlimited money; and (c) no children?

This occurred to me as I was reading the food section of the newspaper recently. As I was looking over the supermarket ads, seeing which stores had the best deals on hot dogs and sandwich-creme cookies, I came across an article saying that nutritionists advise everyone to switch to something they call the "Mediterranean diet." Apparently, the idea is that we should all eat the diet on which poverty-stricken goatherds from the Greek islands subsisted before tourism invaded their paradise. Now they all eat Whoppers with feta cheese, but years ago they roamed the rocky, sunswept hillsides of their native land, eking out a hardscrabble living by tending their goats and sheep and making the hills echo *Opaa!* When they got bored, their diet included such staples as:

Chickpeas, a/k/a garbanzo beans.

Plain yogurt.

Olives, your choice of black or green.

Anchovies.

Bulgur.

Sardines.

Pine nuts.

Raisin wine.

Mmmm, doesn't that make your taste buds stand up and salute? Wait, there's more. You can, should you so desire, *combine* many of these tempting ingredients into a nice main-dish salad or casserole. With a good drenching of sesame oil and coarsely ground cumin seeds. You're only supposed to eat meat a couple times a month. Nothing processed, of course. This, the experts say, is a low-fat, fiber-rich diet that presumably will enable you to live as long as those old Azerbaijani guys in the yogurt commercials and give you the life-affirming outlook of Zorba on a good day.

That's if you actually eat it.

But, as I said, these nutrition mavens are obviously childless. I can imagine concocting, say, a couscous stew and setting it in front of Amanda. "What's this?" she would say, her nose wrinkling at the steaming golden-brown heap. "Couscous," I would tell her, explaining that in the name of celebrating diversity we were having Berber Awareness Night. She gets that diversity stuff at school, you know. I think they alternate Diversity Week with Self-Esteem Week. But Amanda would think "couscous" is a rude name for a body part and would burst into giggles. I can imagine her going to school and telling her little friends, "My mommy made a big koos-koos for dinner last night." And "bulgur"—I don't care to think about what she would do with that.

I used to experiment with this kind of thing, back when it was just the two of us. I have a husband who will eat almost anything. He *prefers* roast turkey, meat loaf, ham, canned fruit cocktail—but he will, in accordance with Scripture, "eat what is set before him." When we were newlyweds, I acquired several shelves of cookbooks and would make such delicacies as quiche with dandelion greens (seriously), turkey-and-squash casserole, brown rice with oranges and curry powder. He would dig in, say, "Mmm, tastes like health" (meaning, where's the salt and sugar?) and dutifully finish his portion. Then he'd go out into the kitchen looking for sandwich cremes.

Once I decided to make pesto sauce. Fresh basil, olive oil, pine nuts whirred together in the blender. It *tasted* okay, but when I poured it over the pasta it looked like, well, green spaghetti, which has all the eye appeal of pond scum. If the good Lord had meant his people to eat green spaghetti he would not have invented red sauce. Even my long-suffering husband could not deal with pond-scum pasta. "Um, I can't eat this," he said. We still laugh about it.

But at least I could *try*, back then. I had the time to look up recipes, shop the exotic-foods section of the supermarket, assemble twenty different ingredients, figure out protein balances. (Is it beans and corn that gives you the protein equivalent of a slab of bacon?) Now, my culinary horizons have narrowed. The short list of what my daughter will eat includes pizza, peanut butter, tuna, macaroni and cheese, most cereals, applesauce, white bread, white-meat chicken, and canned green beans. And that's the stuff that's relatively good for her. She won't eat: most meats, most vegetables, any salads, some fruits. She *certainly* will not eat olives and anchovies. (Neither will I.)

The dietitians keep trying, however. I love those "beyond pb&j" articles in parenting magazines. "Experiment with your kids' school lunches!" they urge. "Get out of the white-bread rut!" They suggest, for example, pita bread stuffed with turkey and sprouts, or open-faced whole-wheat sandwiches with a face of raisins drawn in cream cheese.

They obviously have never sat at a school lunch table. Kids *judge* other children's lunches. Once I sent Amanda to school with a carton of yogurt in her lunch. She came home almost in tears because she had gotten teased for having something *different* in her lunchbox—a spoon. Can you imagine what a child's peers would do with a raisin-face sandwich?

I think it's time the experts cut us mothers some slack. It's taken me this long to wean my daughter from Trix onto Grape Nuts, to convince her that perhaps an oatmeal cookie might be better for her than a Snickers bar. The new guidelines recommend at least eight servings of fruits and vegetables a day. I like fruits and vegetables, and *I* don't eat eight servings. Moreover, what they don't tell you is whether a half-eaten carrot stick or a glass of Juicy Juice counts as a "serving." In my house, it's a serving and that's that. In my house, catsup counts as a vegetable. When you're a parent, you lower your nutritional sights real fast.

Not only that—if you were to follow the Poverty-Stricken Cretan Goatherd Diet and do it right, you'd be in the kitchen most of the day doing earthy, life-affirming things like sorting pebbles out of garbanzo beans. The experts think this is great, but what do you expect? Their idea of a "quick meal" is something that uses twelve different ingredients and takes a mere forty minutes to prepare. My idea of a quick meal is the two minutes it takes to say, "Hello, Pizza Hut? I'd like a large deep-dish to go. With lots of green pepper and onions." (See, we do get our fiber.)

You may infer from the above that I'm getting a little tired of the nutritional do-gooders trying to rob us of our American birthright of Kraft Pasteurized Process Cheese Food (what's the difference between "cheese" and "cheese food"?) and my personal fave—egg-salad sandwiches with lots of mayo lite, red onions, and salsa. If you so inferred, you would be correct. Because, for all her limited, albeit well-rounded, diet, Amanda is rarely sick. The doctor says she seems to be growing okay. I haven't noticed that she's developing rickets or a sallow complexion or anything. And she always gets a good report at the dentist's.

My husband and I are mostly healthy, too. And I know

there'll be a time when I can once again experiment in the kitchen. Amanda's tastes will mature (although maybe not to sardines and pine nuts). I'll be able to devise some vegetarian dishes that really do taste good. I make a great New Orleans-style red-beans-and-rice, for example. Still, it's an uphill battle. The last time I fixed that dish my husband came in, eyed the skillet, and said, "What if you added a hot dog to that?"

TO GRANDMOTHER'S HOUSE WE GO

*M*y mother is selling her house, and she may have a buyer. She wants to move to the ocean, start a new life. The big home place is too much work, too expensive to keep up. Can't say I blame her. But it feels really strange to think that there'll be a new family in her house—in *my* house.

My father had the house built. I lived there from first grade to marriage, and now Amanda loves to visit. She thinks it's a mansion. She gets to sleep in the top bunk of my brother's old bunk beds, play in the funny little knee-level closet my dad created when they built an addition in 1962, sit by the fireplace in the living room while Grandma reads her stories, and look out the window for the deer that venture out of the nearby woods.

I show her the room I slept in when I was her age and tell her how I used to be afraid of the car headlights that would beam into the room and slide slowly over the closet. I thought the lights were trying to find me. I tell her about the times my mother would have ladies in for meetings, and some would come wearing funny little hats, with nets over their faces, and animals around their necks. I show her the place where, driven by some mad imperative, I stabbed a fork into the woodwork one Saturday morning and scratched it and got a licking from my dad with a rolled-up newspaper. This is going to hurt you more than it hurts me. Here, too, is the double bed I used to jump on. Same Beautyrest mattress, a little worse for wear.

I like that continuity.

We have also driven her by the house that *my* grandparents, her great-grandparents, lived in when I was small. I thought it was a magic house. It had a certain smell, as if bread was permanently baking in the ductwork. My grandfather was an executive with Zenith, and they had one of the first color-TV sets. I have told Amanda how we went over there when I was in kindergarten and watched Mary Martin in *Peter Pan*, live from New York, in compatible color! You could turn on the TV by shining a flashlight on it. My sister and I later loved to play Tinker Bell with that light. We watched *The NBC Shower of Stars* and *The Colgate Comedy Hour* and even enjoyed the "fuzz" between channels in color.

Now that I think about it, the reminiscence must sound antique to Amanda, who doesn't remember a time when there weren't computers and VCRs. I must sound like an old-timer maundering on about the first time his horse was nearly run off the road by a Stanley Steamer. (You Know You're Old If You . . . can remember your mother listening to soap operas on the radio— remember steam locomotives like the old "400" that cannonballed down the tracks from Minneapolis to Chicago—remember kids who had odd, twisted legs from polio.)

My grandparents' house had bedrooms all over the place—bedrooms with funny slanting ceilings, bedrooms up a short flight of stairs, a bedroom over the garage, a bedroom off the kitchen. My *great*-grandfather lived there. He was ancient, the oldest person I had ever seen, born two years after Mr. Lincoln was shot. The thought of my balding grandpa having a father seemed impossible, like digging holes in your garden and finding a mastodon femur. Because he had a mysterious dread disease called TB, we children weren't allowed contact with him. I remember his knocking on the window and waving at us when we played in the yard. "Wave," my mother would prompt. I would lift a hesitant small hand, but I was scared of that face. It reminded me of a walnut.

My grandparents' house was full of little surprises, things that made you blink—open this china box and find nonpareil candies; open that can and a cloth snake pops out; peek inside that sugar Easter egg and see a miniature bunny family! My grandparents' house was orange sherbet with little flags stuck in it on the Fourth of July, swinging in a hammock, walking on a nearby golf-course green and seeing a dead bumblebee on the grass. I imagined the bee's getting hit by a golf ball.

My grandparents moved to New York City the same summer we moved into our house. We visited them a couple of times, and they would return to the Midwest occasionally, but it wasn't the same as having a magic house to explore. I missed my grandma, a lot. She was thin and always wore bright-red nail polish—even on her toes—and had a fur coat and drove a convertible. Her name was Cordelia, like a girl in a book. *She*, I thought, *was glamorous*. Unlike my mother, she did not care if I ate my vegetables or went to bed on time. She gave me toys like a battery-operated dog on a leash and taught me the difference between a catbird and a cowbird.

What will Amanda remember about her grandma? Will she come to think of my childhood home as a magic house? Grandparents matter, a lot. Grandparents, I've decided, should never move but should always live just a few blocks away so that their grandchildren can stop in for milk and brownies on their way home from school. Grandparents shouldn't get old and sick and leave you. I would like it if my grandma was still around. Maybe she'd let me borrow her mink.

Now my mother won't even be around. We'll visit her at the seashore, of course, but it won't be the same—not like going back to the home place and trying to show Amanda what life was like back then. No more "This is where my dog Buck followed me to school and I let him into the building and pretended that he snuck in behind me." No more middle-aged-mom going on about how in *my* day there were creeks to wade in and hills to sled on and isn't it a shame that kids can't do that anymore because there's probably a K-mart where once ran a creek, wild and free. Like I was Tom Sawyer. C'mon, Mom, let's go rent a video. Time to move on.

Yes.

I'm grateful Amanda and I had the home place to return to as long as we did. I'm grateful for God's gift of memory and how those memories tend to sweeten with time. But our home place is now here at the corner of Webster and Forest. We don't have as many bedrooms to explore, and no deer come gliding out of the woods. We don't even have woods, unless you count the pile of dead limbs behind our garage. (Even those have their purpose. Once an escaped prisoner ran through the backyards on our block, fleeing police, but was slowed up by our stickery brush pile and captured right across the street. Just call us Crimebusters!) But I'd like to think there's a sort of magic going on here, too, the everyday magic of growing a child.

And anyway, annual free vacations on Cape Cod sound like a pretty good deal to me. I'll bet my mother will even show Amanda a few things on the beach.

HOW TO SURVIVE THE LOSS OF YOUR HAIRDRESSER

I've been abandoned.

I just called for a hair appointment. Naturally I waited too long and am now at the Dire Emergency stage of hair growth, when you call in a hyperventilating panic and scream, "I need a haircut THIS AFTERNOON!" Of course your stylist has nothing for two weeks, by which time you will look like something that needs the services of a scythe.

I never learn. Why, just last week I was examining myself in the mirror and I said to my spouse, says I, "You know, I'm at that teetering-on-the-brink stage with my hair. It's okay now, but soon I'll be over the brink. Better call Holly."

Well, I fell over the brink. Then I called Holly for help. And Holly *wasn't there.*

She had left the salon, the girl told me. Is she working somewhere else? I asked, thinking I would follow her anywhere within the six-county metropolitan area. No, she's going to stay home. She's expecting a baby.

I stood there for a moment. In that instant I went through the initial stages of grief. Numbness: This can't be. Denial: She can't be pregnant. I saw her less than two months ago and she didn't say anything about expecting. Anger: How could she leave me like this?

I groped for words. Uh, when? I asked the girl. Seven months from now. Who's taking her customers? Any one of the stylists here.

So I made an appointment with someone I didn't know and slowly hung up, feeling confused and abandoned, like a child who had been told that her mother had left her and was on her way to Zimbabwe, never to return. Cast adrift. Stumbling through the darkness. I wondered if I should call the salon back and get her home number. Maybe Holly would accept a customer in her home; beauticians do that sometimes. Wait a minute—*I know where she lives!* What if I just showed up, a hairy foundling on her doorstep? She could hardly turn me away, looking like this. I could offer to paint the nursery or something. Give her my old baby clothes. Anything, if only she could still cut my hair.

Only Holly understands my hair. She's given me the best cuts I ever had. People have asked me who did my hair, and I always said, "Holly," serene that she would always be there. She cut *with* my hair, not against it. My hair is thick and wavy and if you cut it wrong, it will rebel and go springing up in strange directions. My hair liked Holly. It does not like everybody. Holly was affordable, Holly was pleasant to talk to. My one pampering was when Holly shampooed my hair. I would close my eyes and feel as though I were at a spa.

Now I don't know what I'm going to do. I have considered seeing if Holly has a secret blueprint for the way she does my hair that she could pass on to the new stylist, the way your former doctor sends your medical records to a new physician. I've even considered switching salons altogether, asking a friend whose hair I admire whom she goes to. But most of my friends complain about their hair. Most people I know don't have hair like mine;

they have nice straight hair that they get permed or keep in a simple short cut. I, however, require the services of a specialist.

And time is running out for my hair. I have to get it done before I leave town in a couple of weeks. I would have to get it done anyway before someone comes at me with a pitchfork or crows start circling, eyeing me for nesting potential.

They say that you need to take risks in life sometimes, trusting God for the outcome. So I guess I'll take a deep breath and prayerfully step into the unknown, submitting myself to The Scissors of the Stranger. Maybe some of Holly's artistry rubbed off on her. Maybe she sat at the master's feet and learned how to sculpt heads. Just in case she didn't, I may do something I haven't had to do in years—bring in a magazine picture and say plaintively, "Can you make my hair look like *this?*"

Life is risk, life is loss. Slowly I have come to the last stage of grief—acceptance. I will survive the loss of Holly. Farewell, dear friend. Blessings on you and your new little one. You're *sure* that you don't want to start a home-based business, maybe while the baby naps? The sound of the hair dryer might lull him or her to sleep. . . .

Well, who knows? Chris, the new stylist, and I may strike up a similar, close relationship. Perhaps she'll give me an even better haircut (although improving on Holly would be like improving on the Sistine Chapel). Maybe someday I'll go in to her—on time—and hear those comforting words, "Just like last time?" Now *there's* earthly security.

IS IT MENOPAUSE, OR AM I JUST HAVING A BAD DAY?

Yesterday morning I awoke with a strange tingling in my fingers. I rubbed them, and the feeling went away. *Probably slept funny*, I thought. But then I remembered what a friend had once told me about how her hands kept falling asleep and someone told her she was having premenopausal symptoms.

At the time, my friend was about as old as I am now. Early forties. In other words, not old. Hardly even middle-aged. (Here is my definition of middle-aged: people a few years older than you.)

But still, I wondered: *Has the tocsin sounded for my youth? Is the sand running out?*

It seems that I find myself losing my temper more than I should, of late. Amanda squirted a water gun at me one night when she was in the bath, and I screamed "STOP IT!" in a shrill voice that was totally unlike me. Is it merely cabin fever, or my old friend PMS, or something new and foreboding?

I've heard that premenopausal symptoms can last a long time before the event itself, that they take many forms. Like right now I'm not feeling very well. I think I'm coming down with the flu that's been going around. I feel a little chilled, a little weak. Think I'm getting a swollen gland in my neck. There's this ache on my arm that comes and goes. I look a little pale. But is it really a virus, or the fact that I stepped in a freezing puddle and I wasn't wearing galoshes, or is it a Sign?

Do I cry more often than I used to? Is that stray hair I tweezed from my face a harbinger of some unfortunate, postmenopausal condition of feminine hirsutism? It can happen, you know. Years ago in *LIFE* magazine I saw a photo of an old sharecropper's wife. She must have been at least ninety, and she had, well, chin whiskers. Being fair-complected, I've never had a problem with any of this. But now . . .

I can't look to my mother for answers. She didn't really go through menopause, because she had a hysterectomy in her forties, and she says now she's just as glad she did not have to endure hot flashes, mood swings, and all the other amusing symptoms of the change of life. She looks great, too.

Change of life. The term sounds like a vast and critical watershed, a continental divide in a woman's existence. One day you have your fresh, moist youth, your hormones, your old rock-and-roll albums, your Cover Girl medicated makeup. Then you pass over this swinging plank bridge over a bottomless chasm, and you wake up, and things are never the same again. Your hair immediately turns gray and wispy, you slap Oil of Olay on your crepey chicken neck, and you start talking tiresomely about how *your* generation scrimped and saved but today's young people all want a free lunch. And, without your hormonal shield, you're all of a sudden vulnerable to old-woman diseases like heart trouble and chronic itch.

Lord, I'm not ready.

Growing up was one thing. As I've already pointed out, there's much to be said for maturity, for leaving adolescence behind. For example, you don't have to take required physical education classes anymore. But I think there's a part of me that has secretly imagined that you grow up and then time stops (like pressing PAUSE on your VCR), and you stay fixed at a certain point—say, around the age of thirty-seven with young children. That seems an agreeable age. You don't just keep getting older and older. *Other* people age, but you somehow manage to escape that fate.

The thing is, I have never quite looked my age. People tend to underestimate by a few years how old I really am. Once a woman said, "You're much younger than I imagined you would be from your writing." (No doubt she was struck by my carefree mien, or maybe it was just the oily patches on my T-zone.) And, because I have a young child, I have always identified with the "young moms," in contrast to some women I know who married while still in their teens, had kids right away, and now, at my age, are starting to think about becoming grandmothers. When I read about people in their early forties having midlife crises, I cannot relate. It took me until forty to figure out what God really wanted me to do with my life. At the rate I'm going I figure I'll hit "midlife" when I'm about sixty.

But attitude is one thing. The inexorability of biology is something else.

It's reassuring, for instance, to know that you *could* bear another child if you want to. I know several women who wonder about that, even women whose children are nearly grown: "Should we . . . ?" Women in their childbearing years. That's me. I've got what it takes. The door to the nursery is still open. I don't want to hear the sound of that door swinging shut forever. I hail from the generation who worshiped at the altar of options, the freedom to choose a spouse, a career, a church, a neighborhood, the idea that life was one big cornucopia, banquet, cafeteria of alternatives— choose your overworked metaphor. *We* were never locked into one job the way our parents were. *We* were free to break from the faith of our fathers and worship where we chose. We're even free to spend thousands of dollars on facelifts.

I'm not worried about lifting my face—yet. And I certainly don't want to turn into one of those women who have had so much plastic surgery that they look like weird effigies, with old eyes staring out from taut faces. You can't disguise the eyes.

Even as I worry about all this, though, I have a disquieting sense that perhaps I shouldn't *be* worrying about all this—*my* body, *my* looks, *my* aging. How, then, does God see the issue? (God: "I was waiting for you to bring Me into it.") Scripture doesn't talk much about menopause except indirectly when God surprises Sarah, who at ninety was "past the age of childbearing," with a son, and Elizabeth, "she who was said to be barren," with a child who would become the Forerunner.

But here! In Philippians, Paul writes that he is "confident of this, that he who began a good work in you will carry it to completion until the day of Christ Jesus" (1:6).

Now, *there's* encouragement! Encouragement, and a gentle reminder that I'm not the architect of my own freedom, the creator of my own choices. God is. That tingling in my hands may mean I'm approaching that rickety swinging bridge called the Change—or it may just mean that I slept lying on my fingers, and I may be facing PMS for years to come. (Talk about your conflicting emotions.)

But, whatever happens, even if that baby-having door swings shut, I'm still not finished. God has more surprises in store, more light to break forth. And, if I have eyes to see His light and ears to hear His voice—even if those eyes are bifocaled and those ears not as sharp as they used to be—I'll be a lot more alive than those ladies with their waxy, lifted faces.

Further, I've decided it *is* the flu, after all. Think I'll go make myself a nice cup of hot broth and wrap up in an afghan.

HOW CAN I BLOOM
WHERE I'M PLANTED
WHEN THERE'S SNOW
ON THE GROUND?

*M*y local newspaper has a comic called *Sylvia*. It's a pretty funny satire of concerns of women in the '90s—and it makes you think, which is sometimes a refreshing pursuit. It sure made me think this morning. Sylvia, who's kind of an armchair commentator, posed the question, "Which one of your New Year's resolutions have you kept?" One woman responded, "I used to have a problem with optimism. I had too much, so I resolved to see my glass as half-empty. It's been a struggle but I'm hanging in there."

I could relate. I could REALLY relate.

Habitual optimists have always annoyed me with their cheerful slogans: "Every day in every way, I am getting better and better" (square *that* with Romans 3:23!). It takes more muscles to frown than to smile. Turn your scars into stars. When life hands you ground chuck instead of steak, make a really tasty meat loaf. Pessimists (I have always preferred to call them realists) always seemed more insightful, more in tune with the reality of the world than shallow optimists. How can we smile when millions of babies are aborted every year, when there's war in Yugoslavia, famine in Somalia, and despair in our own American inner cities? Closer to home, how could *I* make lemonade out of lemons? I'm out of lemons . . . and practically every other foodstuff except spaghetti noodles. It's several days until the next paycheck so supper's going to be spaghetti soup, which I commit by mixing noodles with really old chicken stock (at least I hope it's chicken stock—I didn't label it when I put it in the freezer a few years ago)—and limp celery excavated from the bottom of the crisper. How *can* I bloom where I'm planted? There's snow on the ground. Of course the glass is half empty—there's a crack in it from when Amanda dropped it.

Don't I sound like a delightful guest for your next dinner party?

The problem with chronic pessimism, as the comic strip implies, is that you do have to work at it. For every ray of sunshine that comes your way, you have to conjure up a cloud. If, for example, I receive a nice check for writing a book, I start worrying about the taxes I'll have to pay. If I am enjoying a time of mother-daughter closeness with Amanda, I just know the phone will ring to interrupt the idyll. (Probably the IRS. Have a nice night.) If things are going smoothly in my life in general, I start worrying that I don't have anything to worry about. The pendulum always swings. The bubble always bursts. I echo columnist Russell Baker's sentiment: "In April . . . it is possible to see the world as it might be if only it were not the world."

See, that's it right there: The world always trips you up. You go out your door, it's a balmy spring day, the daffodils are blooming, the birds are whistling at you, and suddenly you remember, *Wait a minute—this is the world*, and your shoulders sag and your step becomes leaden and you go back inside and stare unseeingly at the wallpaper.

This is where optimism gets it all wrong. Optimism places

its hope in the world—in humanity—and placing your hope in humanity is like hoping that the expressionless IRS auditor will buy your laughing explanation about how you were doing spring cleaning and threw away those receipts by mistake and you must have had PMS that day. The IRS will not understand, because the IRS does not get sick. Humanity will not come through. Your husband, your children, fellow believers—even they will let you down.

But God won't. Sometimes I imagine God watching me observe water leaking out of the glass. I imagine His saying, "Okay, worry if you want. But remember what I say to you in my Book. Check out Matthew 6. Oh, and by the way, here's a piece of my grace I'm throwing at you."

And I say, *me?* Why *me,* Lord?

"Oh, just because. Now I want you to pay attention to what I'm doing for you. See that crocus poking up through the soil? Whom do you think did that? Remember how Amanda hugged you last night? Where do you think that comes from? And how about that friend who called you the other day? Any idea who prompted her? Hmmm?"

But . . . we're still strapped.

"Have you already forgotten the deacon who came up to you at church and asked what kind of help you needed? Money? Prayer? Advice?"

Oh, right. That was kind of nice. Okay, then, let's widen the scope. Take Bosnia, for example. The suffering.

A rumble of thunder. *"Don't you think I know all about suffering? How do you think it felt to give up My only Son? I will do what I will do, in Bosnia and everywhere else. Trust in Me."*

Then I am getting better every day? I'll have the perfect life someday?

"I didn't say that. Look, I'm working in you all the time. Would you just leave it up to Me?"

Well, as long as we're talking, could I ask one more thing?

Like why didn't you give me straight hair that I could wear in a fashionably sleek bob? With bangs?

"Fashions come and fashions go. Besides, didn't I tell you I care about every one of those wavy hairs? Now enough. Run along and don't ask any more questions. Job just about wore Me out the other day.

"I'll leave you with one final instruction: Go out again and look at the world. Don't think, Oh, no—not the world again. Try to look at the world and think of Me. And don't you remember what you're always reminding your own daughter?"

What's that?

"What do you say?""

Ah. Thank you.

I may be a slow learner, but I think I'm finally starting to catch on. I'll probably never be one of those perky individuals who finds a bright side to everything—like if you're injured in an accident and your car gets totaled, they insist on saying things like, "Well, it could have been worse. At least the car was totaled in an urban area so that the ambulance and tow truck came right away. Imagine if you'd been out in the middle of nowhere! You could have gotten bitten by an encephalitis-carrying mosquito while you were waiting and no one would have found you for days and you would have been lying by the road with a raging fever *and* a broken leg . . ."

No, that's not me. I've never been perky. I go and whine about having to make spaghetti soup for supper. The difference may be that I'm learning to whine to God, who always listens, always responds, and often sets me straight. And loves me anyway.

That's a relief. All that working at being pessimistic was beginning to get tiresome. Now, if you don't mind, I think I'll go and see if the robins have come back yet.

WHAT TO DO
WHEN YOU'RE NOT
IN THE MOOD

*E*very wife has her own idea about what fans the flames of ardor in her beloved. Some put on romantic music— Michael Bolton, let us say. Some cook a nice dinner with romantic-seeming food like asparagus and strawberries. (No steak; it's too heavy and makes husbands fall asleep.) Some kidnap their mates for a weekend alone. And sometimes the feeling just happens, particularly on those warm, humid days when the air is redolent with flowers and the promise of a really good thunderstorm.

Romance is great. I enthusiastically endorse it. But then there are the romance killers. I myself have been guilty of perpetrating one or two of these things during my fifteen-year marriage. Maybe you have, too. Maybe your husband has. We all make mistakes. But, in the interest of promoting marital harmony, I want to provide you with a list of a few missteps to avoid on the way to conjugal bliss. Let's start with the guys . . .

Men, these are just a few of the things that will turn your wife off quicker than the Off button on the remote:

Renting a *This Old House* video for your just-us-two evening in. Hogging the zapper.

Telling the truth when your wife asks you how she looks, *really*, and it's Saturday morning and she's in that housecoat she's had since 1986.

Buying her an assortment of Rubbermaid products for her birthday. I don't care if you put a bow around the plunger.

Eating salsa right before you kiss her.

Going shopping with her and, in the women's apparel section, hollering, "Hey, Shari-Lynne! The size twelves are over here!"

Doing Three Stooges imitations to your tablemates at the all-church sweetheart banquet.

When your wife asks, "Hon, what do you like best about me?" responding, "You're a good egg," or "You're loyal." Sure, we're loyal, but if that's your first choice in a companion, get a golden retriever.

Ladies, it's your turn. We all like to think we're experts in this department. But we, too, are not entirely blameless. Here are some pitfalls we wives must be alert to . . .

Unlike you, your husband will not ask what you like best about him, any more than he will ask you how he looks. However, if you volunteer such information, do not say something like: "Dear, you know what I like best about you? You're so nurturing."

Making him tuna croquettes when what he really wanted was a porterhouse steak with horseradish on the side. Do *not* remind him of his mother.

If you are enjoying an especially private moment, do not cock your head and say, "Do I hear one of the kids?" This is not the time to remind him that he has children and is, in fact, responsible for their welfare.

Forcing him to lurk in the lingerie department while you try on camisoles. Send the poor guy off to the electronics section.

Elbowing him away when he offers to help you open that recalcitrant pickle jar.

Proposing an arm wrestling match. I don't care how toned you are from aerobics class.

Complaining about him to your best friend.

Being sensible too much of the time.

And finally, a few words of advice to the children. Kids, we love you, but sometimes Mommy and Daddy need some time to themselves. Listen to these tips and we'll all be happy:

Go to sleep. Please. If you can't sleep, lie there and make up a movie or something.

Remember that doors are locked for a reason.

Don't hurry back from the birthday party.

And isn't it about time you took your grandma up on her invitation to visit for a weekend?

STOP THE WORLD, I WANT
TO PLANT A GARDEN

I 've decided it's time to get back to doing some slowing-down things. Insignificant, gentle, taking-time things. I miss them.

Like making bread, or pie. Like hanging laundry. Like planting a vegetable garden. Healthy, farmwifey things where you're using your hands more than your brain.

Early in our marriage there was a period when I wasn't working. It was before Amanda was born. I got into this very domestic period; I had a blue-and-white striped dress that reminded me of a '40s housedress, and I would wear it with a checked apron and feel like a housewife circa 1947 or so, living in some nice, tree-shaded town in Iowa. I had all this time, time to make soup, time to clip recipes, time to rearrange cabinets, time to trim the bushes of the house we were then living in, time to do the laundry just right, sorting and folding, and using bleach. I did everything except enter the Pillsbury Bake-off.

I had a garden, too, a big vegetable garden. Raised everything from onions and peas in the early spring to brussels sprouts and squash in the fall. One year we had all these cucumbers. Couldn't pickle them, they weren't the type. What do you do with excess cukes? Even zucchini is more versatile—zucchini bread, hide 'em in lasagna, that kind of thing.

I sliced some up and tried lying down with cucumbers on my eyes, because I read in a magazine that cucumbers are good for that telltale puffiness. All I got was seeds sliding around my face. But, my goodness, I loved that garden. Loved ordering my Burpee seeds, loved the roar of the Rototiller turning up the earth, loved planting and seeing the first sprouts coming up, loved the peace of it all.

Now my life has changed, mostly for the better but not entirely. My husband does the laundry. Neither of us has much time for it, so we wait until we're wearing ripped underwear and Amanda has to wear too-small pants to school, and then Fritz does these enormous desperation loads of wash, and the electric dryer goes around and around, and so does our meter. I don't clip recipes anymore. I don't even read recipes. I may glance at them, and if they say "Chop" or "Measure" or "Bake at . . ." I toss them aside as intolerably demanding. I don't rearrange cabinets. It's been so long since I looked in some of them, like some of our out-of-reach kitchen cupboards, that I'm not sure what's in them. Cookbooks, I think, and appliances I bought during that early paroxysm of housewifery, like a salad spinner. Imagine, spending money on this huge, hard-to-store device that does nothing except spin-dry leafy greens. Be easier to put them into the dryer drum.

And I certainly haven't planted a garden in ages. Last summer I tried tomatoes, but I didn't get around to it early enough, and it was too cold and they didn't grow and finally Fritz accidentally ran the mower over the poor struggling plants, putting them out of their misery. The housedress has long since gotten ripped up for rags, and in any case it would be two sizes too big now. (All that contented newlywed domesticity has a way of plumping you up.)

But I *want a garden*, preferably one where I can go out

and pick lettuce and tomatoes and peppers and herbs for dinner. I *want* to lug a basketful of wet clothes up the basement steps and hang sheets and towels and shirts on a clothesline on a fresh summer morning, the kind of day when the sun should have a smiley-face on it, like a four-year-old's drawing. I *want* to stand in the kitchen, wearing an apron, and slowly roll out a piecrust. I want to do some sweet, humble, forgotten things. Things you can't hurry through. Things women used to know how to do, and they passed that knowledge on to their daughters and granddaughters. Things that mythical 1947 Iowa homemaker knew how to do.

It isn't just wanting to slow down. It's wanting to do something insignificant.

I'm surfeited with significance. Lately I've been feeling as though everything I do is so intense, so relational, so intellectual, so spiritual, and matters so terribly. My relationship with my daughter—I worry about that all the time. My spiritual life—I'm forever plumbing the depths. My friendships—I put so much into them and analyze them into oblivion. I approach my work with the passion, though hardly the talent, of Handel writing his *Messiah* in a divine frenzy. I ponder the meaning of life. I think about things like how to *really* love my husband.

I'm tired of the stakes being so high in everything I do. I'm tired of always cutting out the unimportant to focus on the *important*. I want to get dirt and flour under my fingernails and forget the clock and not worry how something will be received by an audience. I want to be out of doors in good weather. I think I want to forget myself for a time.

So Amanda and I have been checking out the backyard for a sunny, well-drained patch of earth. She wants to plant carrots, one of the few vegetables she'll actually eat. I want to send beans climbing up the trellis on the side of the garage, and maybe melons, which I've never had much success with. We know a guy at church who has a Rototiller. This may be the year.

I'm going to put up a clothesline, too. Don't see many of those where we live, but I don't care. Anyway, wash on a line suits this old house, where you can still see the little door where coal was delivered. I'll lug out all the blankets and bedspreads and give them a good airing. The smell of a blanket or a sheet after it's been outside on a sunny day . . . well, there's nothing like it.

And talking about smells—bread! Good, honest, oatmeal bread with a salad from the garden. Who cares if it's not perfect? One year it got hot early and the lettuce tasted like jalapeño peppers because lettuce hates heat. I didn't mind. I had done it. God had done it.

Nice, quiet, old-fashioned things. I love the idea, and I think it might be good for me. I'm not sure about rearranging the cabinets, however. The salad spinner will probably stay where it is; I'm not *that* hard up for ways to fill my time. I think I'll be busy enough—but slowly busy.

I WAS GLAD WHEN THEY SAID UNTO ME ...

*H*ow good it is to be here.

I sit in this place, the Lord's place, and look around at the family of God sharing worship. There's Kathy, in the choir. I love the way she always looks as though she is enjoying herself. Tom, ushering, in blue jeans. His wife, Donna, looks so pretty today. Dale and Sue brought their new baby to church. Praise God for what he has done for them! Barb, at the piano. Amanda sits and draws in the children's bulletin. Fritz and I exchange smiles. Everything is as it should be.

A song: *To God, be the glory, great things He hath done . . .* One of my favorites. I'm glad we're singing this—I don't like stumbling through those solemn old Swedish hymns that no one knows. I think the pastors must choose them for the words. Certainly not the melody. There is no melody.

Prayer. Announcements. Someone's wedding anniversary, and everyone claps. A rousing anthem. We do have an accomplished choir. Maybe I should join it next year. No, too much of a time commitment. Scripture, and I realize belatedly that the offertory is next. I try to be as quiet as possible tearing a check out of the checkbook. "And Jesus said, (*r-r-i-i-p*)."

The children are dismissed. Time for the sermon. I settle back with my foot on the chair in front of me. You can do that here, get comfortable in the Lord's house.

It feels so good to relax, ready to take notes. We rushed in at the last minute after a battle to get Amanda out of bed and dressed. My hair is still damp from the shower. I have all this work I've agreed to do. How on earth am I expected to meet all these crazy deadlines? I wish that life were like church—singing, and hearing insightful messages, and smiling at friends. For about three hours out of my week I don't have anything hanging over my head. The wind of the Holy Spirit has blown it all away.

The pastor opens with a funny story. I laugh along with everyone else. I can tell I'm getting the emotional kinks out.

The sermon is interesting. Lots of real-life application. I should really get a notebook to bring to church, like John over there. I'm writing all over the margins of the bulletin and the insert about the denominational program that no one will pay any attention to.

We close with an unsingable hymn. Oh, well. Church shouldn't just be familiar warm-fuzzies; I suppose it's good to try to learn a new song from time to time. But this one goes down when it should go up and up when it should go down. Fritz's voice cracks on a high note, and we both stifle laughter.

Benediction, organ response, postlude. Coffee time! Fritz turns to greet someone from his basketball league. I sit alone for a moment, gathering up my things, watching the people.

What do *they* bring to church, I wonder? Do they arrive in disarray as I do? Are they as relieved to be here as I am? What needs and hurts are they able to lay down for a few sweet hours? What *aren't* they able to release?

I wish I knew more about them. Maybe they wish they knew more about me. Odd. Here we are, God's people. We see one another week in, week out. Sometimes more often, what with meetings, social contact, small groups. So familiar to one another, so strange to one another.

That woman in the corner. She looks so serious. Almost sad. I don't really know her very well. What would happen, I wonder, if I went up to her and said, "You seem down. Can I help?"

There, a man I've hardly ever talked to. He's always friendly, though. Does he like his job? Is he worried about holding onto it? What *is* his job? I don't even know what many of these people do for most of their week.

Here comes a dear friend. Now I know a lot about her—how she became a Christian, what some of her dreams are, but I realize that I have no idea when her birthday is. The names of her siblings. Where she went to college. Basic information, yet we've never shared these things with each other.

What else don't I know? Was she a victim of abuse as a child? Is he involved in an adulterous relationship? Are they desperately worried about money? Does anyone here ever doubt his salvation? Feel like a failure? Harbor festering anger toward her parents?

Oh, every now and then something is revealed, a mask is dropped. When that happens, it feels almost like a sacred moment, as though Christ is breaking in. The body, functioning like the New Testament church. But often enough we keep things light. Why bother other people with my problems? Everybody has enough on his mind. Besides, how would it help?

Once I saw a cartoon titled "It Will Never Happen." Here's something that's hard to picture: What would happen if, at some point in the familiar service, the pastor stepped up to the lectern and said, "Now we're going to do something different"? How would people react if he said, "I know you're all hurting. Paul tells us to bear one another's burdens. What's really on your heart, right now? Stand up and tell us."

Would there be an awkward, shuffling silence? Would it be like the times I've seen in churches when the preacher gives an altar call and nobody comes forward?

Probably at least a couple of people would respond. I can almost guess who they would be.

But would I? And how would the rest of us react to their openness?

I don't know, and maybe it's best that I never find out. There are some hurts—and sins—that can only be healed under a veil of privacy. But it occurs to me now that we are making a beginning. Maybe simply by being here—coming, as the Communion invitation says, "not because you are strong, but because you are weak; not to state an opinion but to seek a Presence"— maybe simply by sitting amid the worshiping community, praying together, singing together, being still before God together—we are in some Spirit-led way laying our burdens on each other.

Then it occurs to me: Maybe someone is here who needs *me*.

Now I disappear into the ladies' room to check my hair. It's finally dry. I can't believe that I sat all through church with its looking like this. I give it a fluff with my brush. And here comes my friend through the swinging door. I can tell she wants to talk. She'll be surprised, but I'm still going to ask her when her birthday is. And maybe a few other things, too.

WHY DO I NEED A PLANNER WHEN THERE'S NOTHING TO PLAN?

*A*m I the only plannerless mom on this planet? The other day I was at a meeting, and discussion turned to arranging some upcoming event. I looked around and noticed that every single person in the room had whipped out his or her pocket calendar, personal planner, total life organizer—you know the kind of thing I'm talking about—and all were consulting their schedules. I sat there empty-handed, smiling vaguely the way people do when they pretend to get a joke.

I really don't get it. Time was when it was good enough to pick up a little complimentary pocket calendar at the drugstore counter every January. No more. I'm seeing these organizers everywhere, toted around by everyday women like you and me. And nowadays most people's planners are more far-reaching and all-inclusive, a veritable window to a life. Many women I know keep a running list of prayer requests in their planners. Phone numbers. Yearly goals. Lists of their core values in life. Calorie counts. Miscellaneous reminders. Books to read. Relevant Scripture verses. Current clothes sizes for all their children, in case they happen to run into a really good sale. Extra pockets for business cards, scratch paper, credit-card receipts, kids' drawings. And on and on.

Let me tell you, planner people hang onto their systems the way some of us hang onto a good compliment. I know a couple of women whose enormous looseleaf organizers are about the size of the black box that, I've heard, is never far from the president, the box that contains the codes for launching a nuclear attack. These women's planners are just as omnipresent and as critical to their survival. Next thing you know, they'll be hiring unemployed teenagers to lug their planners around, much as the president has the one military aide whose sole job description is that of black-box holder.

And it all takes so much time. I've looked at some of these organizers. First, they have all these parts you're supposed to assemble, and I don't do assembly; second, I've watched some people writing things down in their systems, and it looks so labored for something that purports to streamline your life. It reminds me of why my food processor gathers dust in an inaccessible upper kitchen cabinet: During the time it takes to ascertain which blade I am supposed to use at what speed, I can chop a vatful of vegetables with a good kitchen knife.

So I don't use a pocket calendar or life mangement system. I use the freebie wall calendar we get from our insurance man every year. It has pretty pictures of American scenery and hangs in our kitchen by the telephone. The nail is loose in the wall, so it falls off sometimes, and sometimes if you use a felt-tip pen the ink smears. But it's good enough. Anyway, I have the dubious blessing of being endowed with one of those minutiae-cluttered memories that recalls grade-school friends' phone numbers, the theme song from "Mister Ed," and the starting lineup for the 1969 Chicago Cubs. It poses no challenge for me to remember a few dates.

My husband doesn't use a planner either. He has a yellow legal pad, and he writes down everything he plans to do in a given day. *Everything,* from "brush teeth" to "read newspaper" to "lock doors at night." I'm convinced that he will want me to publish his lists anthologized in free-verse form.

Disclaimer: I do not wish to imply that I am somehow delightfully spontaneous and free-spirited because I eschew the drudgery of planners. I may just be too cheap and too poor. Most of my dearest friends swear by them. One day, however, I happened to glance over the shoulder of a guy who was looking through his organizer—and virtually all the pages were blank. Hardly anything was written on them. It was as if his organizer was but a placebo planner, something that comforted him simply by his being able to carry it around.

The incident made me wonder if we all really need to spend forty or fifty or more bucks on ostrich-bound systems with our initials holographically embossed thereon. How did people organize their lives before these things were invented? Didn't they have anything to plan? Did people run futilely about, forgetting birthdays and missing appointments?

Maybe it's just me and my quiet little existence. This may sound like a confession of some fundamental inadequacy, like being born without a digestive system or something, but truthfully, I don't *have* that many appointments. A haircut here, a teacher conference there, an occasional speaking engagement, or business breakfast. Otherwise my schedule runs to the uneventful: write, walk, worry, clean house, go to church, visit Grandma, read to Amanda. Were I to employ a pocket diary, it would read something like this: *Monday at 10:30 A.M.—insert paper in printer. 10:45 A.M.—notice cardinal outside. 11:00 A.M.—examine worn heel on shoe.*

When you think about it, there's a lot of stuff, like planners, that somewhere along the line moved up the charts from "optional" to "must-have." Stuff that I mostly don't possess. Call waiting, to name one. The majority of households I am familiar with have call waiting. I know, because I have been interrupted countless times by that rude little click. (Me to friend: "And then I cried out to God to—" *Click!* Friend: "Hold on.") But such is the power of the must-have mentality that just today I said to my husband, "We really should get call waiting." My husband looked at me and said, "You hate call waiting."

Faxes. Professionals who work at home will, it is said, do untold harm to their careers if they do not purchase a fax machine. (My response to that is, I will do untold harm to my wallet if I *do* purchase one. I also have this suspicion that most of the faxes we got would consist of messages begging us to buy storm windows.)

Disclaimer number two: Do not think I am one of those boring technophobes who giggle about how helpless they are around machines. I work on a computer, which really is mandatory in my business. We have an answering machine, and when I return home and see that red light blinking, it makes me feel happy and wanted.

Still, I can't help wondering where we draw the line with all this stuff we think we can't live without. Stuff that costs money, needs dusting, requires assembly, has to be replaced eventually and may even become obsolete (ask people who sunk money into Betamax video recorders or quadrophonic stereos back in the seventies). Stuff that has to be stored somewhere. Stuff that adds another layer of obligation to your life.

As for me and my house, we shall probably limp along with our yellow lists and the much-anticipated insurance calendar where we compare notes on whose birthday month has a prettier picture. People who call us will continue to be insulted by old-fashioned busy signals. Should I need to send a fax, I shall do what I always do: spend a frustrating afternoon at my church trying to figure out their Reagan-era machine.

But I'll have given myself the gift of freedom—freedom from expensive nonessentials. Freedom to celebrate life! Gee, I'm feeling so spontaneous that any minute now I might burst into song. How about the theme from "Mister Ed"?

WHY MOTHERS
NEED THE FATHER

*O*h, Lord, I did it again.

I had vowed that I would not lose my temper with my daughter. I had vowed that I would not raise my voice. I had vowed that I would not fall apart.

But I did. She got out of bed and wanted something to eat. It was late, a school night. I was tired and on the way to bed myself. And here she was, bounding toward me, saying pertly, "I want some toast." She wanted some toast, and I lost it. My child asked for bread, and I gave her a groan.

As I have said, I come when my child calls. I try to be available to her as I know God is available to me. But I am hardly God. Not even close. I mean, don't even talk about me and God in the same breath. Listen up, my daughter: Believe it or not, I have needs, too. I need rest and refreshment and a life outside you.

Maybe so, but does that excuse my losing control, and not for the first time? Does that excuse my being a poor example to my daughter? (The hammer of guilt always descends when I hear things like "Remember, your children watch what you do, not what you say!")

These are the times when a mother feels really alone.

These are the things you can't talk to your friends about, because you feel so ashamed of yourself. Forget the advice books; according to many parenting experts (especially male parenting experts), if a mom just follows the right system for discipline *and* she herself is always a model of cheer and self-control (*clonk*!), she will raise happy, well-adjusted offspring who will go on to become missionaries, role-model Christian athletes, and presumably, know-it-all parenting experts.

I sank down into a small chair in the corner of the dining room. My dunce stool. The house was quiet, most of the lights turned off. I could hear my daughter tossing in bed. I sat there in the shadows, weeping, trembling, feeling like the living embodiment of Proverbs 15:2: "The tongue of the wise commends knowledge, but the mouth of the fool gushes folly."

How many times can you botch things up before God says, "Okay, kid, that's it. You've reached your quota. I'm not bailing you out this time"? And when you blow it as a parent, the stakes seem so high. There are other people, *precious* little people, involved.

I did not want to compound the felony by letting the sun go down on my anger, so after I had somewhat pulled myself together I went in to my daughter. She was still awake.

"Amanda, I—" I began.

"Mommy, I'm sorry I was so bad," she said sleepily.

Whoa. Hold on a minute. This was not in the script. *She's* apologizing to *me?*

I nestled down next to her and took her in my arms. "Oh, Panda," I said, calling her a name we first gave when all of her really could fit in the crook of my arm. "It's all right. I'm sorry I yelled at you. I was wrong, too. Mommy's going to really try to work on her temper. Now, let's both try to get some sleep. Scoot over a little."

We were both asleep in minutes.

Again and again, I learn something about the love of God through the love of my child. I've struggled for a long time with the tension between law and grace. On the one hand, God does demand our obedience. On the other, we don't have to earn His love. It isn't just a matter of God loves me . . . *if* I toe the mark. Neither, however, is it a matter of, well, I'm saved through faith, so I can go my merry way, botching things up and not worrying about consequences. Justification is not a synonym for making excuses.

No. Because Amanda loves me, forgives me, expects the best out of me, I *want* to do my best for her—and, as she grows up, I see the same process working in her. I see how she responds better to my encouragement and positive expectations than to control and coercion. (Well, usually.)

And because God loves me so much, because in Christ I *have* been forgiven, because my Father picks me up over and over again . . . because of these things, I want to be worthy of His trust. I guess that's what Paul is getting at when he refers to the "Spirit of sonship"—of being adopted by God (Rom. 8:15). To me that's one of the most powerful pictures of His love for us in all of Scripture.

I once worked for a boss who evoked some of these same responses in me, feelings of wanting to be worthy. Although he headed up a multimillion-dollar enterprise and was responsible for maybe a hundred employees, he was never too busy for a how's-it-going periodic visit—and he would really listen. Sometimes he would send me notes commenting favorably on something I had written. He modeled humility and servanthood, and he was not afraid to laugh at himself.

What he did not do was make spirit-trampling comments like, "I noticed you were late the other day," or "You're not working up to your potential." I thrived under this man's gentle tutelage, and I tried to do my best—for the company but also for him.

Not that I continually excelled as an employee, anymore than I continually excel as a mother. I made mistakes. I didn't always work as hard as I could have. But knowing that I could learn from my boss, that I could sometimes go to him and say, "Harold, how would you handle this problem?" helped me to grow. I wasn't toiling on alone.

The night I blew it so badly with Amanda reminded me anew how much parenting is done on our knees, and by that I don't mean scrubbing spilled grape juice or groping under the bed for Barbie shoes. Another thing the experts don't tell you is that mothering is sometimes frustrating, sometimes disheartening, and not always emotionally fulfilling. Recently I worked at our school's book fair, taking money and fumbling with receipts and change. The woman I sat next to at the cashier's table said she was tired, because several nights before she had stayed up all night sewing a Cinderella costume for her fifth-grade daughter. The next day she had to teach.

Moms do crazy things like that, often without much thanks. Nobody gives a mom perks like the Christmas bonuses and corner office I enjoyed in my former life. (An office? Nobody gives a mom privacy, period. That is why bathroom-door locks were invented.)

Some days, too, being a mother makes you sad.

That is why we mothers have to keep turning to the Father—not only to confess our sins and ask forgiveness but also, on a day-to-day, moment-by-moment basis, to say, "Lord, show me how to be a better mother in this situation. Savior, rescue me from my own worst instincts."

Maybe what we need to tell God most is this: "Abba, Father . . . help me to feel less alone. Here I am, your adopted child, and I need to feel Your arms encircling me."

Think about that for a moment. Rest in that image: the Almighty, who flung the Pleiades into the winter sky and can leash Leviathan like a pet, stooping low, in the person of Christ, to put His arms around puny us.

And, as we feel His embrace, we can put our arms around our own children—more confident in our ability to mother them, more certain that we are not alone in this most enormously important thing we are doing.